FRIEDRICH DÜRRENMATT

Friedrich Dürrenmatt was born in
Bern, Switzerland, as the son of a Protestant ....
studied philosophy, German literature and history of art at the
Universities of Bern and Zürich, he began work as a painter and
caricaturist, an interest also evident in the satirical style of his
written work, and as a prose writer, contributing to local
newspapers.

A proponent of epic theatre, his later work included avant-garde
drama, philosophical crime novels, critical essays discussing his
theatrical theories, natural science and politics, and expressionist
plays reflecting upon the recent experience of the Second World
War. Those other plays and radio plays included *Der Blinde* (*The
Blind Man*, 1948), *Romulus der Grosse* (*Romulus the Great*,
1949), *Die Ehe des Herrn Mississippi* (*The Marriage of Mr
Mississippi*, 1952), *Die Physiker* (*The Physicists*, 1962) and an
adaptation of Strindberg's *Dance of Death* as *Play Strindberg*
(1969). In the 1970s he wrote fewer plays, turning to adapting the
works of others in his capacity as a theatre director in Basel, and
towards a prose project (*Die Stoffe*), in which he combined
autobiographical fiction and essays.

Dürrenmatt died in 1990 in Neuchâtel, Switzerland. His work
has been translated into fifty-two languages, and is read and
performed around the world.

'In a world that is losing its mind, his work resembles an outcry
of intelligence' *Le Monde*

'Literary in style, haunting in mood' *Guardian*

'One of the most ingenious, funny and thoroughly apocalyptic
writers of drama and prose of our times' *La Repubblica*

'We have learned in Dürrenmatt's chilling words that what has
once been thought, can never be un-thought' President Jimmy
Carter to the UN General Assembly, 4 October 1977

TONY KUSHNER

Tony Kushner's other plays include *A Bright Room Called Day*; *Hydriotaphia, or The Death of Dr Brown*; *Angels in America, Parts One and Two*; *The Illusion*, adapted from the play by Pierre Corneille; *Slavs!*; *Homebody/Kabul*; *Caroline, or Change*, a musical with composer Jeanine Tesori; and *The Intelligent Homosexual's Guide to Capitalism and Socialism with a Key to the Scriptures*. His translations include S. Y. Ansky's *The Dybbuk*; Bertolt Brecht's *The Good Person of Szechwan* and *Mother Courage and Her Children*; and the libretto for Hans Krása and Adolf Hoffmeister's *Brundibár*, a children's opera for which he wrote a curtain-raiser, *But the Giraffe!*

He wrote the screenplays for Mike Nichols's film of *Angels in America* and for Steven Spielberg's *Munich*, *Lincoln* and *West Side Story* (upcoming).

His books include *The Art of Maurice Sendak: 1980 to the Present*; *Brundibar*, with illustrations by Maurice Sendak; and *Wrestling with Zion: Progressive Jewish-American Responses to the Israeli-Palestinian Conflict*, co-edited with Alisa Solomon.

Among many honours, Tony Kushner is the recipient of a Pulitzer Prize, two Tony Awards, three Obie Awards, two Evening Standard Awards, an Olivier Award, an Emmy Award, two Oscar nominations, and the Steinberg Distinguished Playwright Award. He is a member of the American Academy of Arts and Letters. In 2012, he was awarded a National Medal of Arts by President Barack Obama.

He lives in Manhattan with his husband, Mark Harris.

THE VISIT
or
THE OLD LADY COMES TO CALL

based on the play
Der Besuch der alten Dame
by Friedrich Dürrenmatt

adapted by Tony Kushner

NICK HERN BOOKS
London
www.nickhernbooks.co.uk

A Nick Hern Book

This adaptation of *The Visit* or *The Old Lady Comes to Call* first published as a paperback original in Great Britain in 2020 by Nick Hern Books Limited, The Glasshouse, 49a Goldhawk Road, London W12 8QP

Der Besuch der alten Dame copyright © 1986 Diogenes Verlag AG, Zürich

This adaptation of *The Visit* or *The Old Lady Comes to Call* copyright © 2020 Tony Kushner

Tony Kushner has asserted his right to be identified as the author of this adaptation

Cover image: Photograph of Lesley Manville by David Stewart
Art direction and design by National Theatre Graphic Design Studio

Designed and typeset by Nick Hern Books, London
Printed in Great Britain by Mimeo Ltd, Huntingdon, Cambridgeshire PE29 6XX

A CIP catalogue record for this book is available from the British Library

ISBN   978 1 84842 959 8

A Note on the Play

Friedrich Dürrenmatt's *Der Besuch der alten Dame* premiered at Schauspielhaus Zürich, Switzerland, on 29 January 1956, directed by Oskar Wälterlin, and starring Therese Giehse and Gustav Knuth.

The play transferred to Munich, again with Giehse in the leading role, for the German premiere at the Kammerspiele, and started a tour of triumph from there: first in the German-speaking countries, where it was the most-staged play of 1956 and 1957. It was then produced around the world, in France, Spain, Poland and Japan amongst other countries.

Maurice Valency was a playwright, author, critic, and professor of Comparative Literature at Columbia University, and widely known for his award-winning adaptations of Jean Giraudoux and Dürrenmatt. He adapted the play into English for a memorable production in London and then on Broadway in 1958, starring husband and wife Alfred Lunt and Lynn Fontanne, and directed by Peter Brook. All three were nominated for Tony Awards, and *The Visit* was nominated for Best Play; it was voted Best Foreign Play by the New York Drama Critics' Circle.

Over the years the play has been adapted for the stage and screen many times and in numerous languages. In 1964, Ingrid Bergman and Anthony Quinn starred in a much-altered film directed by Bernhard Wicki – tagline: 'Hell hath no fury...' Here, Zachanassian halts the execution, giving the money to the town as pledged, but forcing Ill (or Miller in this adaptation) to live there amongst his would-be executioners. An opera, adapted by Dürrenmatt himself, with music by Gottfried von Einem, was first performed in 1971, whilst John Kander and Fred Ebb's musical version, with a book by Terrence McNally, opened on Broadway in 2015.

Previous memorable productions in the UK include a 1989
stylised production by Théâtre de Complicité (now Complicité)
at the Almeida Theatre, which transferred to the National, and
Lauren Bacall and Joss Ackland in Terry Hands' 1995
Chichester Festival Theatre revival.

'*The Visit* was my breakthrough,' remarked Dürrenmatt in 1980,
'it is my most popular play.'

This adaptation of *The Visit* or *The Old Lady Comes to Call* was first performed in the Olivier auditorium of the National Theatre, London, on 13 February 2020 (previews from 31 January). The cast was as follows (in alphabetical order):

ROBY	Troy Alexander
MATTIE ILL	Charlotte Asprey
CHIEF SANDOR MUNDZUK	Jason Barnett
DAN	Sam Cox
ANNALISE ILL/JACK E. HOFFMANN	Bethan Cullinane
CHIEF ENGINEER/ BAT GORMLEY	Paul Dodds
MR HOFBAUER	Ian Drysdale
BOBY	Richard Durden
PERCY MUNDZUK	Michael Elcock
LOBY	Paul Gladwin
SHOPGIRL/DANA COWLE	Mona Goodwin
DR JERSEY NUTLING	Garrick Hagon
EDELTRUD HERCKHEIMER/ MRS CREEKY	Liz Izen
MISS HENRIETTA COVINGTON	Sara Kestelman
HUSBAND #7/HUSBAND #8/ TWINNINGS HOON/GYMNAST	Joshua Lacey
CLAIRE ZACHANASSIAN	Lesley Manville
MR EMERSON/ANTONY LEYVANHOUCK/CONDUCTOR	Simon Markey
DOBY	Louis Martin
BILL	Kevin Mathurin
BELSHA/BERNARD MENDELSOHNN	Alex Mugnaioni
REVEREND FERRIS MESSING	Joseph Mydell
ZACHARY ILL	Stuart Nunn
KOBY	Simon Startin

WALLACE	Tony Turner
BEDNEY	Douglas Walker
ALFRED ILL	Hugo Weaving
MRS BLATTER/MRS BALK	Flo Wilson
MAYOR NICHOLAS HERCKHEIMER	Nicholas Woodeson

UNDERSTUDIES

DOBY/ROBY/HUSBAND #7/ TV NEWSMEN	Stuart Nunn
MATTIE/DAN/MRS BLATTER	Liz Izen
ANNALISE/MRS CREEKY/ MRS BALK	Mona Goodwin
CHIEF ENGINEER/ZACHARY/ ANTONY LEYVANHOUCK	Louis Martin
BOBY/LOBY/KOBY/ DR JERSEY NUTLING	Simon Markey
PERCY MUNDZUK/ HUSBAND #8	Troy Alexander
EDELTRUD HERCKHEIMER/ MISS HENRIETTA COVINGTON	Flo Wilson
TWINNINGS HOON/ CONDUCTOR/GYMNAST	Alex Mugnaioni
CLAIRE ZACHANASSIAN	Charlotte Asprey
MR EMERSON	Douglas Walker
BILL/WALLACE	Paul Gladwin
BELSHA/MR HOFBAUER	Joshua Lacey
REVEREND FERRIS MESSING/ CHIEF SANDOR MUNDZUK	Kevin Mathurin
ALFRED ILL	Paul Dodds
BEDNEY/MAYOR NICHOLAS HERCKHEIMER	Ian Drysdale

MUSICIANS
Malcolm Edmonstone, Shane Forbes, Nick Moss, Jo Nichols and Becca Toft

AFTER-SCHOOL TUMBLERS (THE CHILDREN)
Aliya Ali, Ceyda Ali, Georgia Leigh Coleman, Phoebe Rose
Easom, Siahra Edmondson, Tey Tey Edmondson, Harry
Heaslewood, Rio King, Lexi Grace Kowlessar, Katie Mitton,
Willow Mitton and Asha Sthanakiya

SUPERNUMERARIES
Rhyanna Alexander-Davis, Auriane Amor, Jessie Baek, Karl
Best, Jules Chan, Karen Connell, Thea Day, Sophie Dessauer,
Holly Freeman, Keletso Kesupile, Elham Mahyoub, Genevieve
Osili, Martha Pothen, Sabrina Richmond, Vinesh Veerasami and
David King Yombo

CHOIR
Ese Adjekughele, Amelia Anderson, Tony Bannister, Ali Blows,
Louise Boyd, Grace Cowie, Sarah Cribdon, Flora Dawson,
Miranda Ford, Laura Glover, Neil Gordon, Alan Gribben, Amy
Hendry, Hannah Horsburgh, Jack Hudson, Georgia Ingham,
Rebecca Jeetoo, Zanna Mercer, Jo Monowid, Laura Beth
Mortemore, Daisy Mouatt, Lou Nyuar, Natalie Panto, Victoria
Priest, Kira Rogers, Natalie Sanderson, Kate Sketchley,
Cameron Slater, Hannah Smith and Clarence Tan

Director	Jeremy Herrin
Set Designer	Vicki Mortimer
Costume Designer	Moritz Junge
Lighting Designer	Paule Constable
Movement Director	Aletta Collins
Composer	Paul Englishby
Sound Designer	Paul Arditti
Music Director	Malcolm Edmonstone
Choir Leader	Clare Wheeler
Company Voice Work	Jeannette Nelson and Victoria Woodward
Dialect Coaches	Danièle Lydon and William Conacher

Staff Directors	Eva Sampson and Sophie Moniram

Originally commissioned by and produced in association with David Binder.

THE VISIT

or

THE OLD LADY COMES TO CALL

Characters

WALLACE, *an unemployed man*
BILL, *an unemployed man*
BEDNEY, *an unemployed man*
DAN, *an unemployed man*
BELSHA, *a painter*
MRS BLATTER, *a bankruptcy manager*
MAYOR NICHOLAS HERCKHEIMER, *Mayor of Slurry*
MISS HENRIETTA COVINGTON, *Principal of Slurry High School*
REVEREND FERRIS MESSING *of the First Reformed Methodist Church*
ALFRED ILL, *a shopkeeper*
CLAIRE ZACHANASSIAN, *a billionairess*
BOBY, *Mrs Zachanassian's butler*
HUSBAND #7, *a handsome Greek owner of Brazilian plantations, married to, then divorced from Mrs Zachanassian*
CHIEF ENGINEER *aboard the Inverary–Oswego–Toledo Mistral Express*
THE MIXED-RACE CHOIR
PERCY MUNDZUK, *Chief Mundzuk's teenaged son*
DR JERSEY NUTLING, *Slurry's town doctor*
CHIEF SANDOR MUNDZUK *of the Slurry Police Department*
DOBY, *a convicted and condemned murderer and Mrs Zachanassian's sedan-chair bearer*
ROBY, *a guitar-playing convicted and condemned murderer/light tenor and Mrs Zachanassian's sedan-chair bearer*
THE AFTER-SCHOOL TUMBLERS
EDELTRUD HERCKHEIMER, *the mayor's wife*
HERCKHEIMER GRANDCHILDREN
FOUR PALLBEARERS, *immensely tall women dressed in black in Mrs Zachanassian's entourage*

FRENCH MAIDS, *at least forty of them, in Mrs Zachanassian's entourage*

TWO LARGE-CAT HANDLERS, *both women, in Mrs Zachanassian's entourage*

A PANTHER

KOBY, *a fat funny little man in Mrs Zachanassian's entourage*

LOBY, *a fat funny little man in Mrs Zachanassian's entourage*

MATTIE ILL, *Alfred Ill's wife*

ZACHARY ILL, *Alfred Ill's son*

ANNALISE ILL, *Alfred Ill's daughter*

HUSBAND #8, *a French absurdist playwright, briefly married to, then returned by Mrs Zachanassian*

MR HOFBAUER, *Slurry's town butcher*

MRS BALK, *a regular customer in Ill's shop*

MRS CREEKY, *a regular customer in Ill's shop*

MR EMERSON, *a regular customer in Ill's shop*

STATIONMASTER, *a recent hire*

CONDUCTOR *aboard the southbound Blasdell–Fredonia–East Palestine–Pittsburgh Sirocco*

SHOPGIRL *at the Grab and Go*

TWINNINGS HOON, *reporter for* Life *magazine*

ANTONY LEYVANHOUCK, *photographer for* Life *magazine*

BARNARD MENDELSOHNN, *reporter for the* Saturday Evening Post

DANA COWLE, *CBS television reporter*

BAT GORMLEY, *NBC television reporter*

JACK E. HOFFMANN, *ABC television reporter*

CAMERA OPERATORS, *and* SOUND, LIGHTING, MAKE-UP *and* WARDROBE CREWS *for CBS, NBC and ABC*

A GYMNAST

THE CITIZENS OF SLURRY

The play takes place in 1956, in the town of Slurry, New York.

This text went to press before the end of previews and so may differ slightly from the play as performed.

ACT ONE

Scene One

A hot afternoon in early autumn. A railroad station, built in the early 1920s, a time of prosperity. There's a cute little Gothic Revival brick stationhouse, slatted benches flanking the door. In front of the stationhouse, two platforms divide four sets of train tracks – local and express. The local tracks are those nearest the stationhouse. The express tracks are located just past the downstage edge of the stage, in the audience. There's a station clock on the local platform, mounted atop a rococo cast-iron pole.

A flyspotted, faded cardboard sign on the door announces that the stationhouse is 'CLOSED' and 'THE STATIONMASTER WILL RETURN BY', beneath which there's a printed clock without hands. The station clock has both its hands but the hour hand hangs limply down, pointing permanently at 6, while the minute hand spasms uselessly between 50 and 51. Slats are missing from the benches; missing glass from the stationhouse windowpanes has been replaced with plywood; the glass of the display case for the railway schedule is cracked and the schedule lies curled up inside at the case's bottom. The tracks are almost entirely obscured by weeds. Here and there on the walls of the stationhouse, obscenities both verbal and graphic have been timidly graffitied.

On a chipped enamel sign above the stationhouse door, the name of the town, which apparently is

SLURRY

though the sign is in the process of being eclipsed by the large banner that four men, WALLACE, BILL, BEDNEY and DAN, hoist up in front of it. BELSHA, a painter, stands to one side with a paintbrush tied to a very long pole in one hand and an open can of red paint in the other, an old paint-splattered ladder folded on the ground at his feet.

The BANNER-HOISTERS *interrupt their effort at the first warning vibrations of an approaching express train; all five* MEN *follow the speeding train as it passes the station from left to right, making a tremendous din, raising a wind in its wake that blows the banner all about. The* MEN *stare at the train long after it's vanished from sight and hearing. The banner flutters to the ground, a tangled mess. Then:*

WALLACE. The Zephyr.

BILL (*nodding*). BBD&O's fastest.

WALLACE. Pittsburgh to Augusta in under a day.

BEDNEY. Remember when it used to stop here, Tuesdays northbound, Thursdays south.

BILL. All the express trains stopped at Slurry. Not anymore.

DAN. There was that one time, the Zephyr pulled in and out popped ZaSu Pitts! And that man, that –

BEDNEY. No, ZaSu Pitts came through here once alright but –

DAN (*continued from above*). What was his name?

BEDNEY (*continued from above*). – she came in on the Erie-Superior's Tramontana, Cleveland–Cheektowaga–Hamilton–Ontario.

The four MEN *start to straighten out the banner, talking as they do:*

BILL. The Tramontana, right, and the Willywaw, the Sirrocco –

WALLACE. Oh, the Sirrocco, I remember her!

BILL (*continued from above*). – the Bayamo, the Warm Braw and the Squall, the Brubru and the Haboob and –

BEDNEY (*to* DAN). Slim Summerville.

DAN. Right! Slim Summerville and ZaSu Pitts for the Western New York premiere of Hal Roach's *Niagra Falls* at the Slurry Sidereal Panopticon. Mischa Ellman set a world record for 'The Flight of the Bumblebee'!

BEDNEY. Fifty-three seconds if I'm not mistaken.

DAN. *Here. Right here in Slurry.*

BILL. Bertrand Russell on the subject of Ethical Mathematics. Blackstone the Magician and his Levitating Donkey. Billy Graham's Crusades!

WALLACE. This town of ours was once a destination! Now it's a by-water, bypassed by postwar commercial abundance. Every last one of our factories: closed! The town's coffers, bone dry! No work, no hope, no future, no –

BELSHA. I studied with Glackens of the Ashcan School! I came to Slurry in search of a subject to paint, and I found it! Here! In the hills of pig-iron ingots behind the Place-In-The-Sun Amalgamated Smelting Plant, I found grim realism but with idiosyncratic coloristic inclinations! And here I've remained, watching helplessly as the war's artificial economic dynamism departed with the arrival of peace and all the goddamn plants closed one by one –

BILL. I was the best turn-key project manager Bockmann's ever had! Then one day, no warning, Bockmann's is in receivership, next day shuttered up, and what am I now? Nothing!

DAN. Join the club! My whole life I worked for Place-In-The-Sun Smelting. (*To* BELSHA.) I used to eat my lunch sitting on them pig-iron hills! All gone now, sold for scrap or God knows, and I get my lunch from the soup kitchen at the church.

BELSHA. A SERIOUS POLITICAL ARTIST and *look* at me, painting a welcome-home banner for the world's wealthiest parasite!

Another express train roars by. The men hang on to the sign. The train passes.

WALLACE. Camden & Amboy Extraterritorial Nor'Easter, Hagerstown–Altoona–Belfast–West Seneca.

DAN. We're alive now only in the sense that moss and lichen are alive. Why?! What happened to us?!

WALLACE (*tapping the side of his nose*). Dark unfathomable forces at work. About which I need say no more. Now, let's hoist this banner like we been promised we'll eventually get paid for doing.

They resume their work hoisting the banner. They get it taut enough to be legible:

WELCOME CLAIRIE!

It spreads open. Offstage, nearby, a screech of brakes and the pneumatic hiss of bus doors opening, followed by a bus driver's voice: 'SLUUUUUURRRYYYY!'

MRS BLATTER, a haggard-looking bureaucrat in a rumpled overcoat and discouraged hat, enters dragging a huge, heavy, beaten-up documents case.

Behind her, offstage, the bus doors hiss shut as the driver calls: 'DUNKIRK! ANGOLA! EDEN! BUUUUUFFALLO!' and the bus drives away. MRS BLATTER watches it leave. Then she turns to look at the banner, which the MEN are tying in place. As BELSHA sets the ladder up in front of the sign, MRS BLATTER points to it and asks:

MRS BLATTER (*reading the sign*). 'Clairie'? That's a tetch informal, isn't it?

They stare at her.

When's she arriving?

WALLACE. Clairie? The 5:19 p.m. local.

BELSHA *has started to climb the ladder.* MRS BLATTER *says to him:*

MRS BLATTER. That ladder looks rickety. The town's insurance has lapsed and creditors have seized the treasury, so good luck trying to sue.

BEDNEY. And who might you be?

MRS BLATTER. Blatter. Bankruptcy manager.

The five MEN look at her.

BILL (*to* MRS BLATTER). Bankruptcy?

DAN (*to his friends*). The buzzards are circling! (*To* MRS BLATTER.) Slurry may be down but don't count your chickens! We got an ace we ain't played yet!

WALLACE (*pointing at the sign*). Richest woman in the goddamned world!! Born here in Slurry! And she's coming home! Today!

BEDNEY. You read about those hill towns she visited in Italy last summer?!

MRS BLATTER. I didn't.

WALLACE. Just motoring through! On a whim she retired their debt! *And* she built 'em a women's hospital! State-of-the-art!

BEDNEY. And yachting through the Dardanelles, in Patras, Kalamata and Argos, raggedy kids on every street corner, apparently, so in her wake she left behind a chain of nurseries!

WALLACE. The Zachanassian Centers for Infancy Enhancement! Endowed in perpetuity!

MRS BLATTER *nods, then goes into the stationhouse. The* MEN *continue regardless, caught up in telling these stories.*

DAN. *Can you fathom her money?*

WALLACE. The Armenian oil monopoly, railways, radio stations, armaments, pesticides, polyvinyl chloride plants and –

BILL. She drew her first breath right here in Slurry!

BEDNEY. Slurry's got toddlers! And women to be hospitalized!

WALLACE. Why else would she come back? Nobody visits Slurry! Not anymore!

DAN. I bet you she smells profit in retooling the Reverberatory Aluminum –

BILL *sees something approaching. He whistles a quiet alarm to the others:*

BILL. Look sharp, fellas, it's the Welcoming Committee.

The four MEN *snap to various kinds of shabby attention as* MAYOR NICHOLAS HERCKHEIMER, *mayor of Slurry, enters with* MISS HENRIETTA COVINGTON, *Principal of Slurry High School,* REVEREND FERRIS MESSING *of the First Reformed Methodist Church, and* ALFRED ILL, *a shopkeeper.* DAN *salutes the* COMMITTEE, *who pay him no notice.* BELSHA *begins painting a new exclamation point.*

MISS COVINGTON (*as she enters*). We don't know her denominational preference, Reverend, or if indeed she has any religious beliefs at all –

MAYOR HERCKHEIMER (*to* ILL). You recall what church her family went to?

ILL. It was too long ago. We didn't spend a lot of time discussing theology.

MAYOR HERCKHEIMER. You're sure she'll remember you? It's understandable, exaggerating your connection with someone that rich and famous, but under these highly charged circumstances, it'd be unfortunate. We're counting on you to –

ILL (*sharp!*). We were close as it gets. It's just I don't remember God ever coming into it.

MISS COVINGTON *has been looking at the sign. She calls up to* BELSHA:

MISS COVINGTON. I think *two* exclamation points might convey desperation.

BELSHA (*working, muttering*). Critics.

MISS COVINGTON. And, I don't know, 'Clairie'? What if she prefers to be addressed as Mrs –

MAYOR HERCKHEIMER. 'Clairie' was my idea and I like it! Let the rest of the world genuflect to Claire Zachanassian, billionairess! In her hometown of Slurry she's our little Clairie Mugler.

ILL. Mucker.

MAYOR HERCKHEIMER. *Mucker?* What the hell kind of a
name is –

REVEREND MESSING. Her father was Mucker the contractor.

WALLACE. He built the bleachers for the football stadium.

BEDNEY. My son broke his clavicle when they collapsed.

BILL. An incurable alcoholic, Mucker was.

BEDNEY. Not only a drunk: a *mean* drunk.

REVEREND MESSING. His wife fled. I encouraged her.

ILL. Yeah. She left Claire behind.

REVEREND MESSING. She hoped the child would have
a steadying influence on Mr Mucker.

ILL. He beat Clara on a daily basis, until the DTs got the better
of him and they carted him off to the loony bin in Utica.
Screamed himself to death.

*There's a moment of silence; no one knows what to say.
Then:*

MAYOR HERCKHEIMER (*glowering at* ILL). I mean you
make it sound as if she was miserable when she lived here!
But she must have affection for, for something in Slurry or
she wouldn't return. Did she like roaming in the woods?
Wasn't she happy here?

ILL *laughs, involuntarily.*

ILL. Sorry, it's just… She didn't roam much, we went to the
pine woods with a purpose. And when the weather was bad
we'd go to Peterson's barn – Happy? She was only happy
when we…

A moment, lost in himself, then he shakes it off.

What she was though was tough as old tree roots, scary
sometimes.

MAYOR HERCKHEIMER *stares at* ILL, *a beat, then turns
to* BELSHA:

MAYOR HERCKHEIMER. 'Welcome Mrs Claire
Zachanassian.' We're presuming an intimacy that –

BELSHA. The sign's finished. As ordered.

MAYOR HERCKHEIMER. We'll pay for the correction, just –

BELSHA. With what money?

MAYOR HERCKHEIMER. What's that supposed to –

A stationhouse window opens. MRS BLATTER *sticks her
head out and says to* MAYOR HERCKHEIMER:

MRS BLATTER. The very man I've been looking for.

MAYOR HERCKHEIMER. Hooray.

MRS BLATTER. The marble countertop at the ticket window?
Is that the town's property or the railway's?

MAYOR HERCKHEIMER. The railway's.

MRS BLATTER. It's the town's, isn't it.

MAYOR HERCKHEIMER *is defeated.*

Come help me unscrew it.

WALLACE. Do it yourself.

MRS BLATTER. I work for New York State. I have a
discretionary budget.

DAN. We have wrenches.

Brandishing wrenches, they file into the stationhouse.
MAYOR HERCKHEIMER *turns to* ILL:

MAYOR HERCKHEIMER. You've got to help us, my boy –
I've done the best I can, marshaling every last tatter of our
severely exhausted resources to make Slurry seem
redeemable, the kind of place a sane woman worth
uncountable quantities of money might decide to sink even an
infinitesimal fraction of that money into. I'm hoping our pluck
and grit can still shine through – the After-School Tumblers
will escort her from here to the hotel, somersaulting all the
way, the Mixed-Race Choir will bring up the rear, the

Kanatsiohareke Tribe from the Mohawk reservation have agreed to do their Rabbit Dance on the Concert Green for her, and the firehouse bell will ring when she –

MRS BLATTER *opens the door of the stationhouse*.

MRS BLATTER. We sold the firehouse bell last week to a bell collector in Antwerp, Ohio.

MAYOR HERCKHEIMER. The church bell, then!

REVEREND MESSING. The Antwerp collector bought that as well.

MAYOR HERCKHEIMER. You, you sold *the church bell*?!

MRS BLATTER *holds the door as the four* MEN *file out, carting a long grayish-white marble countertop. As the others watch it carried off:*

REVEREND MESSING. It was sell the bell or close up shop for good. As goes Slurry, so goes Slurry First Reformed Methodist Church. Attendance is down. Everyone blames God for the money drying up, since no other explanation is available.

MAYOR HERCKHEIMER (*back to* ILL). No bells then. But at tonight's banquet in her honor, the 4-H-ers are remounting their pageant, *Hay, Hogs and Pigs*, and after supper the Rotarians are planning a sparkler display. The Shriners in their fezzes will –

DAN. Ask the Shriners who stole our money.

BEDNEY. Freemasons! (*Whispering*.) They're in cahoots with the Jews.

MISS COVINGTON. Desperation is no excuse for stupidity. Did I teach you nothing?

BILL (*to* MISS COVINGTON). Who was it abolished the gold standard?

MISS COVINGTON. The U.S. Congress! And what's the gold standard got to do with our –

WALLACE. Who controls Congress?! The Freemasons, that's
who!

MAYOR HERCKHEIMER (*to* ILL). Ill! Ill! Listen to them!
They're horrible! There's no disguising it with tumblers and
sparklers! Who in her right mind would have the slightest
interest in helping *them*?! This is one of those awful moments
when we're forced to be honest: We're *unattractive*! Nothing
is less attractive than human need. Slurry's future's in Mrs
Zachanassian's hands, and our only shot at getting her to
extend those hands in aid and succor, Ill, is you. Think hard,
think back, remember what you were to her or vice versa or
something, anything that constitutes a thread from here to her,
some claim you have on her affections!

ILL. I have no claims on her affections! I never said I did!
Maybe once, years ago. But, but that was –

MAYOR HERCKHEIMER. No buts!! If she doesn't carry a
flame or at least a smoldering ember of feeling for you, my
boy, the whole town's good as dead. Everyone says you were
sweethearts, up to all kinds of hijinks in the –

ILL. It was forty-five years ago! I was nineteen, she was
seventeen, we were stupid kids, we went out together a few
months. The town's cooked up this 'Romeo and Juliet
legendary love' angle, I never said we were in –

It was that we both came from really poor families, or, *I* was
from a poor family, she wasn't from anything. You felt bad
for her, or, or leastways I did. I tried being nice to her, and
she… responded, and she was, oh, man, to me she was…

He laughs to himself.

She was one of those girls you can see at night when there's
no moon to light her, she carried light inside, maybe, or
maybe because I always *wanted* to see her so bad, I never
knew it but I think my eyes opened wider to take in the
moon she carried in her belly, like she was the world's
prettiest witch. Never saw skin like hers, I knew it'd burn
me; nor hair like hers, sparkling, even in the dark. And her

body was thin, springy, whiplike and liquid like a willow branch, she was like flux and molten iron mingling, flowing through the dark, trailing sparks like stars, like fire'd just laid herself down in the mildewed hay in Peterson's barn, or in St Konrad's Forest, burning on the needle beds beneath the candlewood pines, and she let me in, we... adhered, her and me, breath and sweat and heartbeat, and then...

He's silent, heavy. Then a shrug, and then, quietly:

Life told us it was time to go our own ways. The way when you're young life still talks to you and tells you: 'Do things.'

A beat. MAYOR HERCKHEIMER *smiles, claps* ILL *on the back, then:*

MAYOR HERCKHEIMER (*to* BELSHA). 'Clairie' is exactly right.

A train's horn a far distance away.

BEDNEY. That'll be the Mistral, the Inverary–Oswego–Toledo express.

BILL. Rockets past us at 3:07 p.m.

MAYOR HERCKHEIMER. I'm sorry to press you so hard on these points of your private, personal hoodads and fadiddlings, Ill, but –

ILL. Don't worry about it, Mr Mayor, it's –

MAYOR HERCKHEIMER. – but when you're mayor, you'll do what you must for the sake of your town.

The train is getting nearer, so everyone speaks louder.

ILL. [When] I'm what now?

MAYOR HERCKHEIMER. Once the billionairess refills the pension fund I'm retiring and who'd be more electable than our town's savior's most cherished local memory, our hometown shopkeeper? To whom, my dear boy, will Slurry be more indebted than to you?

ILL. But I'd be a lousy mayor, I don't know thing one about running a town.

MAYOR HERCKHEIMER. You don't need to understand town management, you can hire others to do that. You only have to understand indebtedness: it's what weaves the threads of humanity into the whole cloth of community. Get the people in your debt and you've got an unbeatable asset come election day!

The express is approaching at great speed, its powerful engines thunderously loud.

BELSHA (*shouting*). Need someone to design campaign posters?

DAN (*shouting!*). NEED A CAMPAIGN MANAGER?

BILL (*shouting louder*). DRIVER?

BEDNEY (*even louder*). OFFICE STAFF?

MAYOR HERCKHEIMER (*yelling*). YOU'VE GOT TO BE *CONFIDENT*, ILL, YOU GOTTA STOP THIS APOLOGETIC MOPING, LIKE YOU'RE A PRISON SENTENCE IN SEARCH OF A CRIME! BECOME THE HANDSOME RECKLESS BOY YOU USED TO BE AND I DON'T DOUBT HAVE REMAINED IN CLAIRIE'S MEMORY, AND OUR FORTUNE'S GOOD AS –

MAYOR HERCKHEIMER *stops as the howl of the onrushing express train is abruptly interrupted by a hideous shriek of massive brakes, metal screaming as it skids over metal. Finally, a gigantic HISS and steam and dust roll in, enshrouding the petrified* SLURRIANS. *From within the cloud:*

WALLACE. Well, I'll be goddamned.

BILL. The Mistral!! It, it –

BEDNEY. The Inverary–Oswego–Toledo express!

DAN. It *stopped*. In Slurry. Holy jumpin' Jupiter!

WALLACE. The Mistral stopped here!

The cloud disperses as:

CLAIRE ZACHANASSIAN *enters.*

It is impossible to know her age. Her face, heavily painted, almost resembles a mask from some ritual drama. She's bedecked with alarming jewelry. She is terrifying, excessive to the verge of insanity, also improbably beautiful. She walks with the aid of a jeweled cane.

Following CLAIRE ZACHANASSIAN *is* BOBY, *her octogenarian butler; he always wears impenetrable black-lensed sunglasses. Behind* BOBY, CLAIRE ZACHANASSIAN*'s* HUSBAND #7, *handsome, elegant in expensive angler's waders, fishing rod in hand.*

CLAIRE ZACHANASSIAN *gazes about, apparently unaware of the* SLURRIANS, *who stare at her, dumbstruck.*

Without looking at WALLACE *or anyone else, as if addressing the air,* CLAIRE ZACHANASSIAN *asks:*

CLAIRE ZACHANASSIAN. This is Slurry?

WALLACE. It's, it's –

CLAIRE ZACHANASSIAN (*to* BOBY). Oh, Boby. It's Slurry. It's as awful as I remember it. St Konrad's Forest is over that hill, there's a brook that runs through the trees, you can catch trout in it –

ILL (*quietly, in a near-trance*). Clara.

At the sound of his voice, she freezes and stops speaking.

CLAIRE ZACHANASSIAN (*not looking at* ILL). Oh look! (*Pointing.*) That towering protuberance poking above the trees! That's the silo by Peterson's barn.

WALLACE. It's, it's, you're, you're –

It's Claire Zachanassian.

(*To* CLAIRE ZACHANASSIAN.) You're Claire Zachanassian.

SLURRIANS (*entranced*). Zachanassian.

WALLACE (*suddenly electrified!*). IT'S CLAIRE ZACHANASSIAN! IT'S CLAIRE ZACHANASSIAN! IT'S CLAIRE ZACHANASSIAN!

The assembled SLURRIANS *lose their shit, running about, screaming variations of 'It's Claire Zachanassian!'*

MAYOR HERCKHEIMER (*over the above*). No, no, we're not ready, we're – The tumblers! The Welcome Parade! My morning coat! My grandkids! The Welcome – no wait I said that already! (*To* BELSHA.) You're blocking the banner! (*To* BILL *and* BEDNEY.) Move the ladder! He's blocking the banner!!

BILL *and* BEDNEY *rush to the ladder and start to collapse it.* BELSHA *grabs on to the ropes securing the banner, clinging to the top of the ladder with his feet.*

BELSHA. What are you doing?! I'm gonna – It hasn't dried, you'll smudge it to shit!

REVEREND MESSING (*over the above, to* DAN). Run! Run to town! Tell them she's here, she's here!!!

BILL (*over the above, to* BELSHA). *Leggo the goddamned ladder!*

DAN (*over the above, to* REVEREND MESSING). The Mistral doesn't stop here. It's not supposed to stop till Oswego.

BEDNEY (*over the above, to* BELSHA). *Get down, Belsha! You're spoiling her sign!*

REVEREND MESSING (*continuing from above*). Fetch the Mixed-Race Choir from the social hall, tell them to hoof it to the station, on the double, they're rehearsing in the – She's here! She's here!

BELSHA (*over the above*). *You let go of the ladder, you're gonna break my –*

DAN *gets the message and runs towards the town.* MAYOR HERCKHEIMER *calls after him:*

MAYOR HERCKHEIMER. Tell my wife to fetch my hat! My coat! The grandkids!

The Mistral's CHIEF ENGINEER *stumbles in, nose and forehead bloodied, his red hat in his hand, shock giving way to murderous rage.*

CHIEF ENGINEER. You, you, you pulled, the the –

CLAIRE ZACHANASSIAN. The emergency brake.

CHIEF ENGINEER. This, this is a, a, it's an express!!
Passengers aren't allowed to, to pull the –

CLAIRE ZACHANASSIAN. I wanted to get off. The train had
to stop first.

CHIEF ENGINEER. *You nearly derailed us! There could have
been a massive, massive wreck! People might have DIED.
(Turning to* MAYOR HERCKHEIMER.) ARE YOU IN
CHARGE HERE?! This woman, she, she pulled the
emergency brake! I want her arrested! She –

CLAIRE ZACHANASSIAN. Arrested? You're thick, aren't
you? (*To* MAYOR HERCKHEIMER.) It boggles the mind,
doesn't it, how nowadays they'll hire certifiable morons for
any position. (*To the* CHIEF ENGINEER.) I already
explained myself, fathead: I wanted to stop here, and the
train wasn't stopping. What are brakes for? What was I
supposed to do? Jump off an express train going seventy
miles an hour? I'm not young anymore, not enough for
stunts like that. (*Indicating her right leg*.) See this leg?
Artificial. (*Indicating the other leg*.) This one too. Artificial.
Parts of it anyway. Most of it. Hips as well, but what
business is that of yours, the point is: What kind of a cretin
expects first-class passengers to jump off a speeding train?

CHIEF ENGINEER. You take the local if you want to, to –

CLAIRE ZACHANASSIAN. The local? That stops at every
dispiriting little slum from Wirt to Penn Yan, glum fat
farmwives occupying every sprung upholstered unsanitary
seat, gnawing at rancid sausages with rotted stumps for teeth
oh and now look, you've upset me. (*Turning to* BOBY.)
Boby, give this importunate creature whatever sort of bribe's
required to make him and his locomotive go away.

From an elegant little satchel BOBY *produces a large stack
of fresh cash tied in a red ribbon and holds it out to the*
CHIEF ENGINEER, *who stares at it transfixed, as is*

everyone other than CLAIRE ZACHANASSIAN, *all attention riveted to the money.*

CHIEF ENGINEER. But this, but this must be, there must be ten thousand…

SLURRIANS (*entranced*). Ten thousand!

The CHIEF ENGINEER *snatches the money and starts to count it.*

CLAIRE ZACHANASSIAN. Boby, he doesn't get it, he's still here. Double the bribe.

BOBY *produces another stack, and hands this to the* CHIEF ENGINEER.

CHIEF ENGINEER. But what for…?

CLAIRE ZACHANASSIAN. The Railroad Widows and Orphans Fund.

CHIEF ENGINEER (*at a total loss, staring at the money*). The *what*?

BOBY (*loud, in a decidedly creepy, if not to say unearthly voice*). RAILROAD WIDOWS AND ORPHANS FUND.

CHIEF ENGINEER. But, but there isn't a Railroad Widows and Orphans Fund.

CLAIRE ZACHANASSIAN. Tell your wife and kids, they'll set one up. (*To* MAYOR HERCKHEIMER.) You have that air of sham authority, can't you get rid of this pest?

MAYOR HERCKHEIMER *moves towards the* CHIEF ENGINEER, *when suddenly the* CHIEF ENGINEER, *looking from the cash to* CLAIRE ZACHANASSIAN, *goes pale, bug-eyed and slackjawed.*

CHIEF ENGINEER. Oh my God. Oh my God. You're Claire Zachanassian. (*To the* SLURRIANS.) She's Claire Zachanassian. (*To the money.*) It's Claire Zachanassian. (*Bursts into tears of shame and joy.*) God keep you, Angel of Mercy, Spirit of Kindliness… (*Blows his nose into the money, then:*) May I wait for you, after you're done here, I'll take you any place, any place you –

CLAIRE ZACHANASSIAN. Thank you, no. I don't know how long this visit will take.

HUSBAND #7 (*whiney*). But Mousey-Mouse, you said we'd head to the Finger Lakes by sunset.

CLAIRE ZACHANASSIAN (*to* BOBY). He's whining again, Boby. It's giving me regrets.

As BOBY *leans in to whisper to* HUSBAND #7, *who swats him away:*

There's a church in Slurry with a fresco of the Last Judgment I used to brood over as a girl, in the Catholic church, in the bad part of town, I want to see it again. And I mentioned trout, Boby: tell – (*Gesturing irritably towards* HUSBAND #7.) I said go fish.

HUSBAND #7. But Catkin, if the train leaves it'll take away the press car with all the reporters and photographers.

CLAIRE ZACHANASSIAN (*to* BOBY). Tell him I don't want reporters, Boby, or no, stop talking to him, it encourages him. Tell the inexplicably lingering engineer to make tracks before the shock from our unscheduled stop wears off and the press start to disembark. Take them to Oswego. They'll scuttle back here soon enough.

DAN *has returned and is helping the frantic* MAYOR HERCKHEIMER *don his official outfit. In the distance, the* MIXED-RACE CHOIR *is heard running to the station, singing 'I Wonder Who's Kissing Her Now?'*

BOBY (*to the* CHIEF ENGINEER). Double-time.

(*To* HUSBAND #7.) Go fish. (*Flapping his hands as if shooing a fly.*) Go.

HUSBAND #7 *blows a raspberry at* BOBY *and does not budge. The* CHIEF ENGINEER *exits towards his train, bowing backwards to* CLAIRE ZACHANASSIAN *over and over as he goes. The* MIXED-RACE CHOIR *enters helter-skelter at a trot, choir robes hiked up.* MAYOR HERCKHEIMER *gestures to them to stop singing, which anyhow they're doing badly, flustered and winded as they are.* MAYOR HERCKHEIMER *turns to* CLAIRE ZACHANASSIAN:

MAYOR HERCKHEIMER. Dear Clairie Zacha–

The express train kicks into high gear, the station bell rings, the train's horn blasts, ear-splittingly loud. More SLURRIANS *enter, cheering, all of them dressed in cheap, ugly clothing, or dignified old clothing that's now threadbare; some are downright ragged.*

MAYOR HERCKHEIMER'*s speech is drowned out, but he keeps talking, undaunted, as the Mistral thunders off.*

During all of this, CLAIRE ZACHANASSIAN *has scanned the crowd of* SLURRIANS *until she finds the face she's looking for. She fixes* ILL *with an unreadable stare. He responds by wincing painfully and staring at his feet.*

MAYOR HERCKHEIMER'*s done, and now the train's noise subsides.*

CLAIRE ZACHANASSIAN (*staring at* ILL). What a speech. So many words. Thank you, Mr Mayor, for pronouncing every one.

ILL *finds he can't raise his head to look at* CLAIRE ZACHANASSIAN. *Finally,* MAYOR HERCKHEIMER *clears his throat in a loud hurrumph directed at* ILL, *who looks up at* MAYOR HERCKHEIMER. MAYOR HERCKHEIMER *indicates* CLAIRE ZACHANASSIAN; ILL *finally turns to her and says softly:*

ILL. Clara.

CLAIRE ZACHANASSIAN. Alfred.

ILL. Thanks, very much, for, for visiting. Us.

CLAIRE ZACHANASSIAN *looks away from him.*

CLAIRE ZACHANASSIAN. I've been aching to do this for oh so many, many, many years. Since last I left Slurry behind me. But no one ever really leaves, anyplace, anything, don't you think? Alfred?

Alfred.

What do you think, Alfred?

ILL (*very nervous*). It's just… terrific you made the time, I mean took the – I mean found time to –

CLAIRE ZACHANASSIAN. You mean the time has come. Have I been in your thoughts? From time to time?

ILL (*a beat, then:*). You know you have. Clara.

CLAIRE ZACHANASSIAN. I know. And the Gods know how much you've been in mine, how I dwell upon those days when we were as one, together.

ILL (*a smile breaking out*). Yeah. Yeah. They were… unforgettable, those –

ILL *stops himself. She's not looking at him; he feels sick. He looks panicked at* MAYOR HERCKHEIMER, *who tries as subtly as he can to indicate 'KEEP GOING, GO ON.'*

Clara, I –

CLAIRE ZACHANASSIAN. No. Not that. My pet name. My animal name.

ILL (*a beat; reluctance, embarrassment, and something else he can't identify; then:*). Vixen. My needle-nosed little vixen.

CLAIRE ZACHANASSIAN *growls a low, surprisingly deep, slow growl.* ILL *approaches a few steps and says, quieter, more confident, more intimate:*

My captive feral cat.

CLAIRE ZACHANASSIAN *purrs like a very old cat; it turns from a purr to something like a snore, or the sound of a large, dangerous, wild boar.* ILL *steps back, shocked. Then:*

CLAIRE ZACHANASSIAN. And…? Got anything else?

ILL *looks at her, then a little grin breaks forth: She's up to her old tricks. Even more quietly, more intimate:*

ILL. The world's prettiest witch. My witch. My magic. Mine.

CLAIRE ZACHANASSIAN. And I called you my Alley Cat, my Midnight Tom.

ILL. I'm still a prowler. I'm still dark.

CLAIRE ZACHANASSIAN (*finally looking at him*). You're kidding yourself. Your hair is dyed – incompetently, I might add –

ILL. They, they made me do that, they said it'd be a good idea to –

CLAIRE ZACHANASSIAN. – and you're too fat to prowl, they'll hear you coming now, the lady cats in estrus, the little-bitty kittens, you're easy to evade, and you drink. A lot. In private. I can always spot a lonesome drunk. Probably explains the flab.

ILL, *with some difficulty, absorbs the insult and the aggression. Then:*

ILL. You won't get an argument from me. But you. You're the same vixen as ever you were.

They stare at each other.

CLAIRE ZACHANASSIAN. I'm old as you, fat as you, and my right leg was sliced off in a pileup on the Rio Bravo coastal road in a heavy fog, we'd been smoking… God knows what, and I alone am left to tell the tale. My left leg's gone, first cancer, then a dueling accident with sabers, some flesh that's still mine but mostly manufactured. Want to kiss the fleshy bits, Alfred, or I'll let you lick my leg the way you used to. It's sterling silver, it blackens so Boby has to polish it, but it can stand up to spittle.

ILL (*starting to sweat*). That's – Is that really so? Well, see, I… didn't know… that, but –

He sways as if he might faint. MAYOR HERCKHEIMER *moves to stand right behind him.*

CLAIRE ZACHANASSIAN (*gesturing in the direction of* HUSBAND #7). This is my husband. #7. (*Without looking at him.*) Husband #7, meet Alfred Ill. We played together. When we were young. Husband #7 owns... something agrarian, farms, tobacco farms. Plantations, really. Are you married, Alfred?

ILL. Well, I –

CLAIRE ZACHANASSIAN. But isn't it funny, because a moment ago, when I offered you my legs, cancer-cankered, scarred, inorganic as a, as an axe, a knife, a shiv, a machete, when I said you could lick me I'd swear, married as you must be, I could practically hear your glands lubricating your lips with anticipatory drool, as if I was your wife and *you* were my husband instead of poor old – (*To* BOBY, *indicating* HUSBAND #7.) His name!? His name! I can't –

BOBY. Moby.

CLAIRE ZACHANASSIAN. Right. Moby. Right. His *actual* name's Pedro, or anyway it's Spanish, and since my butler's name is Boby, I thought it'd help me remember what to call him. Husbands aren't so durable, or for that matter, *en*durable, husbands wax and wane, so I change their names to match my butler's. (*Gesturing to* HUSBAND #7 *without looking at him.*) Moby, bow to Alfred.

HUSBAND #7 *bows.*

He's really sexy, isn't he? Everyone tells me he is. And just because he's gorgeous, it doesn't mean he can't think. Watch this: (*Turning to* HUSBAND #7, *in a voice of sharp command.*) Moby! Think!

HUSBAND #7 *grimaces.*

Deeper! Deeper thoughts!

HUSBAND #7 *grimaces, as if in some sort of severe gastric distress, his knees buckling slightly, his torso concaving.*

Dropping his fishing rods, his hands seem to be clawing at something in the air before him.

Good! Now even deeper than that! Really, really deep! Do it!

HUSBAND #7 (*grunting out his response*). I... can't... Cat... kin...

CLAIRE ZACHANASSIAN. Aw, come on, baby, try, make Momma proud, *come* on...

HUSBAND #7. But... if I... try... any harder, I... I might... soil myself again... and –

Fortunately, the station bell rings. The spell is broken. HUSBAND #7 *falls to his knees, spent.* CLAIRE ZACHANASSIAN *stares off again.*

CLAIRE ZACHANASSIAN. It's amazing, isn't it, Alfred? The mind-body problem. Spinoza wrote in Portuguese, didn't he? I knew, but I've forgotten. And Moby's Brazilian, isn't he, Boby?

BOBY. Greek.

CLAIRE ZACHANASSIAN. Then he can't be called Pedro, that's not a – But yeah, you're right, I wanted a Greek Orthodox wedding, the white domes, the blue sea, the iconostasis bedizened with entirely unfamiliar saints. Honestly, it was disappointing. Oh Ill, what can you do seven times without habituation rendering it dull? My whole life, maybe only our cat-clawing, over and over and over till we'd flayed one another, but it never got stale.

He starts to respond but she cuts him off.

My *Spaziergang* down the *via dolorosa* that runs through Slurry will begin right here – (*Pointing.*) the railyard shithouses. My father worked on them. During a brief and extremely rare sober interlude. My nose tells me they remain in use. He brought me here to watch him work, when I was little; as I said, he wasn't drunk, so for practically the whole time he worked on them he knew that I was his daughter. Afterwards he'd forget, and I'd come out here to hide from him; climb up on the roof, spit on the customers. I'd spit for hours, but only on the men.

Pointing to PERCY MUNDZUK, *in the last row of the* MIXED-RACE CHOIR.

That tall boy in the back, in the bass-baritone section, with the, the long neck and the protuberant Adam's apple. He's got a voice!

MAYOR HERCKHEIMER (*to* PERCY). You! Kid! Come here!

MISS COVINGTON (*also to* PERCY). Hurry up! This is no time to dawdle!

PERCY *makes his way from the back of the* MIXED-RACE CHOIR *to the front and stands before* CLAIRE ZACHANASSIAN, *insolent, aware of his attractiveness.*

CLAIRE ZACHANASSIAN. Do you have parents?

PERCY. 'Course.

MISS COVINGTON *slaps the back of his head.*

MISS COVINGTON. Yes, ma'am!

CLAIRE ZACHANASSIAN (*to* MISS COVINGTON). Don't slap him! You're his teacher! Let others slap him if he's bad. (*To* PERCY.) Do you think you're bad?

PERCY *smirks and shrugs.*

Do you like money?

PERCY. Sure.

CLAIRE ZACHANASSIAN. What does your father do?

PERCY. Cop.

CLAIRE ZACHANASSIAN. Does *he* like money?

PERCY. Likes it like anything.

CLAIRE ZACHANASSIAN. Does he know how to wink at sin?

PERCY. Uh, not sure I – *What?*

REVEREND MESSING. He that winketh with the eye causeth sorrow, as the –

CLAIRE ZACHANASSIAN (*to* PERCY, *loud enough to shut up* REVEREND MESSING). I confused you, it's alright, I asked you a hard question about your daddy, now run as fast as your long legs can carry you and find him and ask him: Can he wink at sin?

PERCY *stands there, still confused.*

(*To* BOBY.) He remains confounded, he needs to be shouted at, Boby.

BOBY (*screaming at* PERCY). *GO!!!!*

PERCY *runs off in the direction of town.* CLAIRE ZACHANASSIAN *turns to* REVEREND MESSING.

CLAIRE ZACHANASSIAN. Is your church the one with the Apocalypse fresco?

REVEREND MESSING. No, Madame Zachanassian, mine is the First Reformed Methodist Church –

CLAIRE ZACHANASSIAN. That mean you don't offer last rites to dying men?

REVEREND MESSING. I, I comfort them, as best as I can.

CLAIRE ZACHANASSIAN. I'm sure. What about a rapist and murderer who was sentenced to death?

REVEREND MESSING. Ah. Yes, well, that's – Ha ha. But I can't recall anyone having been executed in Slurry.

CLAIRE ZACHANASSIAN. Not yet.

(*Calling out.*) Is there a doctor in the house?

An elderly man, DR JERSEY NUTLING, *steps forward from the crowd; he carries a doctor's satchel.*

MAYOR HERCKHEIMER. This is our local doctor, Dr –

CLAIRE ZACHANASSIAN. Dr Nutling, as I live and breathe.

DR NUTLING. It's my absolute pleasure to meet –

CLAIRE ZACHANASSIAN. We've met.

DR NUTLING. We did?

CLAIRE ZACHANASSIAN. I came to you to cure me of my affliction. I was sixteen. It was 1910, illegal, I'd've found the money somehow, or you could've let me pay later, the desperate can't help but conceive of the extension of credit as mercy in monetary form, which it never is but that's irrelevant because my desperation made no impression on you, cash on the barrel you said; it was quaint. And mean. And apparently for you, forgettable.

DR NUTLING. I can't say that I can recall… What was wrong with you?

CLAIRE ZACHANASSIAN. Ill remembers.

(*To* ILL.) You'd remember if you'd paid for it like you said you would.

ILL (*almost inaudible*). Clara… I was… I didn't have any –

CLAIRE ZACHANASSIAN (*to* DR NUTLING). You still fill out death certificates?

DR NUTLING. I'm a board-certified pathologist.

CLAIRE ZACHANASSIAN. I had no money, I had nothing back then, I couldn't pay, so it all came out in the open, my disease, everybody knew, except my daddy, who in the midst of it all came home from the crazy house in a rough pine box. (*To* DR NUTLING.) Daniel Mucker. Remember his corpse?

DR NUTLING. I do, indeed I do! Cirrhosis was the cause of death, I remember that because it had brought about a rather startling condition, gynecomastia, he had these –

CLAIRE ZACHANASSIAN. He'd grown breasts. Like a woman's. It was… mythological.

DR NUTLING. A drunkard's liver can't synthesize hormones, y'see, and –

CLAIRE ZACHANASSIAN. What do you charge for death certificates?

DR NUTLING. Three bucks for the original, a dollar fifty per copy.

CLAIRE ZACHANASSIAN. Cash upfront?

DR NUTLING. 'Course.

CLAIRE ZACHANASSIAN. And if a person died from this or that and I wanted his certificate to stipulate heart attack and – (*A look at* ILL.) say he was flabby, so that would be plausible: How much to put down heart attack as cause of death?

No one speaks. Then:

I'm ready to begin my tour.

MAYOR HERCKHEIMER *gallantly offers her his arm.*

I can't walk all that way! I wasn't kidding about my legs! Every step is agony.

She gives BOBY *a barely perceptible signal; he blows into an inaudible whistle that starts every dog for many miles barking and howling. Then two hugely muscled young guys enter, greasy pompadours, black leather jackets over tight white T-shirts, embarrassingly tight blue jeans and black motorcycle boots, one with a guitar slung over his broad back; both chew gum. They carry between them an old, magnificent, gilded baroque sedan chair.*

This is Doby, and the other one's Roby. They're from California. San Quentin in fact, they were scheduled for the gas chamber but I paid to have their sentences commuted to life and then I bought the parole board.

DOBY *and* ROBY *lower the chair. She climbs in. They hoist it.*

(*To* BOBY.) Bring the luggage to the hotel, and don't forget: the coffin gets a room of its own.

MISS COVINGTON. The coffin?

CLAIRE ZACHANASSIAN. In case one's required. I support local businesses but I heard your only undertaker went under.

(*To* DOBY *and* ROBY.) Head for the silo, boys, and the
woods beyond.

DOBY *and* ROBY *carry the sedan chair off just as the*
AFTER-SCHOOL TUMBLERS *tumble in, covered with
dirt, thistles, dead leaves, followed by* DAN, *followed by*
MAYOR HERCKHEIMER*'s wife,* EDELTRUD
HERCKHEIMER, *carrying* MAYOR HERCKHEIMER*'s
hat and fancy coat, followed by the* HERCKHEIMER
GRANDKIDS *holding bedraggled bouquets, all panting
from running.* CLAIRE ZACHANASSIAN *notices none of
this, staring ahead or out at the audience.*

ILL *stands alone, deep in thought.*

The SLURRIANS *start to follow, cheering, but it stops at the
arrival, from the direction of the stopped train, of four*
PALLBEARERS, *very tall, very powerful women, dressed in
black, veiled in black, wearing black stovepipe hats banded
with huge black ribbons; they carry a large black coffin. The*
CROWD*'s cheering dies at the sight. They part to make way
for the* PALLBEARERS, *who pass by silently, heading for
the town. They are followed by an apparently endless
procession of formally dressed* FRENCH MAIDS, *each
balancing on her head a piece of luggage, each piece
different from the piece before. During this:*

WALLACE. The grand old days are back again!

BEDNEY. Fame and fortune have alighted, gracing our town!

CHIEF SANDOR MUNDZUK *arrives, with* PERCY *right
behind him.*

CHIEF MUNDZUK. Where's the billionairess?

REVEREND MESSING. Borne aloft toward silo and sylvan
glades. She *is* like one of the graces, isn't she?

MISS COVINGTON. There's nothing especially graceful about
her, she's more like one of the Fates, less a Claire and more a
Clotho, who spins the threads of human life and was
sometimes worshipped as the Goddess of Necessity –

*The parade of trunks, suitcases and boxes concludes with
two women* LARGE-CAT HANDLERS *in heavily padded
suits carrying between them a large cage in which a black*
PANTHER *paces, growling its weird high-pitched growl at
the* SLURRIANS, *who first applaud, then scatter in terror
when the* PANTHER *stands up and they realize the cage is
open on top.*

MAYOR HERCKHEIMER. Holy hell! (*To* CHIEF
MUNDZUK.) Is that, that –

MISS COVINGTON. It's a panther.

MAYOR HERCKHEIMER. I know what it – That cage is
manifestly inadequate!! (*To* CHIEF MUNDZUK.) *It'll get
loose!! IT'S A PANTHER!!! DO SOMETHING!*

CHIEF MUNDZUK. Like what? I can't shoot it.

MAYOR HERCKHEIMER. Of course you can't shoot it, it's
her pet!!!!

CHIEF MUNDZUK. She'd fire me.

She hired me.

MAYOR HERCKHEIMER. She did not!

PERCY. Good as.

MAYOR HERCKHEIMER. She can't! You're the only cop
we got.

CHIEF MUNDZUK. Because you laid off everyone else.

The PANTHER *has been carried off in the same direction as
the luggage. The* CROWD *reassembles, watching it go.*

BEDNEY. I suggest we go together, all of us all as one at once;
we'll intimidate it. Safety in numbers.

MISS COVINGTON. Not a bad suggestion; panthers hunt by
isolating their prey from the pack.

The CROWD *tightens into a cluster and starts to move
apprehensively in the direction of the town.*

From offstage, the PANTHER's *shuddering, menacing cry. The* CROWD *stops.*

WALLACE (*showing his forearms*). Look. Goose pimples.

MISS COVINGTON. Also: Panthers have an aversion to loud noises.

The MIXED-RACE CHOIR *bursts into Jule Styne and Frank Loesser's 'I Don't Want to Walk Without You' and the* SLURRIANS *exit, tight together.* MAYOR HERCKHEIMER, ILL, CHIEF MUNDZUK *and* PERCY *remain.*

MAYOR HERCKHEIMER. She's headed for Peterson's barn. She wants to wander in St Konrad's Forest.

ILL. She didn't ask me to go with her.

MAYOR HERCKHEIMER. So? She didn't say don't. She's revisiting your trysting places, man, what in the name of solvency are you waiting for?!

ILL. I'm *married*, for Christ's sake. And, and she's... I mean –

MAYOR HERCKHEIMER. *Dulce et decorum est pro patria mori.*

ILL. She used to hide from me, back then, I mean really hide, in awful places – waste bins and open graves, there she'd be, curled up, trying not to breathe, like I was some killer looking to –

But I always found her.

She knew I would. I think she knew.

He walks off, slowly. MAYOR HERCKHEIMER *watches, then turns to* CHIEF MUNDZUK.

MAYOR HERCKHEIMER. Follow him, make sure he –

CHIEF MUNDZUK. I don't work for you anymore.

MAYOR HERCKHEIMER. What about your boy?

CHIEF MUNDZUK. He's a kid!

PERCY. How much?

MAYOR HERCKHEIMER. Whatever we paid your dad.

CHIEF MUNDZUK. Don't want him exposed to anything unsavory.

MAYOR HERCKHEIMER (*to* PERCY). Just tail him till he gets to her. If he strays, come find me. (*To* CHIEF MUNDZUK.) It's lovers reuniting, it's *Romeo and Juliet*, what's unsavory about that?

MAYOR HERCKHEIMER *exits*.

CHIEF MUNDZUK. If they get up to anything Scandinavian, cover your eyes.

PERCY. Sure thing, Pop.

PERCY *smirks and sprints towards Peterson's barn, nearly colliding with* KOBY *and* LOBY, *two funny fat little men, both in dark suits, dark hats and very dark glasses, who wander in from the direction of the train platform, holding hands.*

What, are you blind?!??

KOBY. As you surmise, sir.

KOBY *and* LOBY *laugh*.

PERCY. Just watch where you're going!!

PERCY *runs off*.

CHIEF MUNDZUK. Where'd you two come from?

LOBY. Inverary–Oswego–Toledo–City of Dis!

CHIEF MUNDZUK. Where's Dis?

KOBY. Next door to Dat!

CHIEF MUNDZUK. You… You work for her? For Mrs –

LOBY. The old lady owns us.

KOBY. She holds us.

LOBY. In Sheol she controls us.

CHIEF MUNDZUK. Me too, I work for her too, I think so anyhow, she said she's gonna hire me –

KOBY. She hires then blinds you.

LOBY. Blinds you then binds you.

CHIEF MUNDZUK. What the hell are you talking about!?

KOBY (*screaming, to* LOBY). *WHAT THE HELL ARE WE TALKING ABOUT?*

LOBY. *ABOUT HELL!! WE'RE BLIND!*

KOBY. *WE'RE BLIND!*

CHIEF MUNDZUK. Oh. Oh, yeah. Sorry, I –

KOBY. Take us to town?

CHIEF MUNDZUK. Oh! Uh, sure, I – Good you can laugh in spite of your, your situation. Come on, it's this way.

LOBY. Thanks, Officer, ever so much.

KOBY. Ever so, Officer.

LOBY. Officer, much!

CHIEF MUNDZUK. Hey! How'd two blind guys make out I'm a cop?

KOBY *and* LOBY. Smell of your leather.

LOBY. Your leather, together with Dis, Dat –

KOBY. – and the Other. Smell of your boots.

LOBY. Fat boots, flatfoot!

CHIEF MUNDZUK. I don't get it. What're you supposed to be, some kinda comedians?

KOBY *and* LOBY *go into a vaudeville routine, complete with soft-shoe, singing:*

KOBY *and* LOBY. WE'RE KOBY AND LOBY! WE'RE KOBY AND LOBY! WE'RE THE OLD LADY'S!

CHIEF MUNDZUK. She doesn't mind you calling her that?

KOBY. Who knows her mind?

LOBY. Only the Gods know; we don't:

KOBY. We're blind!

They laugh.

CHIEF MUNDZUK. I admire your pep. I'll laugh too if she pays me to do it!

KOBY *and* LOBY. She shall! You will!

They exit.

Scene Two

St Konrad's Forest, among the candlewood pines. Cool and green-shadowed, the floor a blood-red bed of aromatic needles. Birds sing.

ROBY *sits in the sedan chair, softly strumming something melancholy and sweet on his guitar, while* DOBY *sits on the forest floor, eyes closed, probably dozing.*

CLAIRE ZACHANASSIAN *and* ILL *go separately from pine tree to pine tree, examining the trunk of each tree, looking for something.* CLAIRE ZACHANASSIAN *examines the bark cyclopically through a large monocle,* ILL *unaided except for a late-middle-aged squint. As they hunt, they talk:*

ILL. They cut down the valley pines past East Aurora, all the way to Attica Prison, it's all meadow now, but they spared the candlewoods, there's talk of a bird sanctuary. Maybe you should buy it up!

CLAIRE ZACHANASSIAN. Never cared for birds. Except as dinner. Ortolans you blind and fatten and drown in brandy. Or chickens that come home to roost.

ILL. Anyways, I know it's still here, my kids have seen it.

CLAIRE ZACHANASSIAN. Ah, your kids!

ILL. Boy and a girl. Teenagers.

CLAIRE ZACHANASSIAN. You married that girl you were sniffing around, the one with the weekly allowance?

ILL. Mattie Grimke.

CLAIRE ZACHANASSIAN. Grimke! Right! (*Doing a radio advertiser's voice.*) Brought to you by Grimke Automotive!

CLAIRE *and* ILL (*radio advertiser's voice*). Chautauqua County's number-one retailer of Ford cars and trucks!

He laughs. She doesn't.

ILL. Mattie's brothers torpedoed the business; old man Grimke died, then one of the brothers lost his oldest boy in the war, and –

CLAIRE ZACHANASSIAN. Aren't you old to have teenaged children?

ILL. We waited a long time.

CLAIRE ZACHANASSIAN. To procreate, or to consummate?

ILL. Clara, that's not any –

CLAIRE ZACHANASSIAN (*continued from above*). The former, I imagine, you never cared for kids, whereas for the latter, I can't imagine you waiting long for that; unless she's frigid? Or repulsed by you?

(*Calling.*) Doby! Henry Clay!

DOBY *jumps up, then saunters over, reaches deep inside his front jeans pocket, pulls forth a long black cigar-shaped leather tube and proffers the cigar inside to* CLAIRE ZACHANASSIAN, *who takes it, rolls it, rips off an end with her sharp white teeth, and spits the end onto the forest floor. As she's doing this,* DOBY *takes a box of matches from his back pocket and holds it open before* CLAIRE ZACHANASSIAN.

*She takes a match, strikes it, lights the cigar and then throws
the lit match onto the pine needles at her feet. The needles
instantly catch fire.* CLAIRE ZACHANASSIAN *ignores the
fire;* DOBY *giggles;* ILL *rushes over and stamps it out as*
CLAIRE ZACHANASSIAN *resumes her scrutiny of the trees.*
DOBY *follows her, box of matches still open.*

ILL. Careful now! These needle beds are dry! You can't fling lit
matches on –

CLAIRE ZACHANASSIAN *turns back to* ILL, *takes
another match from the box, lights it and flings it at him,
then another lit match, then another and another and
another.* DOBY *giggles as* ILL *frantically stamps around,
snuffing out the flames.*

ROBY (*to* DOBY). Hey, dig it, it's Smokey the fuckin' Bear!

ILL (*over the above, to* CLAIRE ZACHANASSIAN). Clara!
Cut it out! Goddamn it, what're you thinking?!

CLAIRE ZACHANASSIAN (*to* ILL). Fire. Hell. The usual.
What are you thinking?

ROBY (*playing and singing, softly*).
You just have to look around you
And you'll find it's not a joke,
To see what you'd be missin'
If they all went up in smoke.

ILL. I'm thinking how I've been in hell since the day you left.

CLAIRE ZACHANASSIAN. And I left and became hell itself.

ILL. You're upset. You're upset with me. But, but look at me!
What I've become! If I hadn't turned you loose, you'd've
stayed and been ground to rubbish like me.

CLAIRE ZACHANASSIAN. Are you rubbish, Alfred?

ILL. Her old man wouldn't let me in on the car franchise, so with
her dowry we started a downtown grocery store, but
downtown's a ghost town now, my customers are on relief, the
go-getters moved to look elsewhere for work. The woe-is-me's

I cater to shoplift if I turn my back. I have nothing. My life's
a bad joke.

CLAIRE ZACHANASSIAN. Your children must comfort you.

ILL. Hah! They hate me because I'm broke. They don't know
the value of anything.

CLAIRE ZACHANASSIAN. They'll learn, soon enough.

ILL. I think about you, all the time, Clara, not because your
name's always on the radio and your face keeps popping up
on the TV news. I think about how tricky life can be, how
I did you dirt, I know, but then again I did you right, didn't I,
you fled this broken-down dump of a town like you were one
of the up-and-at'emses, which we both know you weren't.
I drove you forth, into the world, and now you know the
world, the entire world, and –

CLAIRE ZACHANASSIAN. I own it. An alarming percentage
of it, anyway. But I can't forget this forest, these trees, the
heart you gouged out of that sapling's tender skin, with A
and C inside, how our letters bled, in long sticky ribbons
running down the bark, ants and ladybugs caught in the flood
of amber sap, suffocating entombed in such aromatic
opulence. I've wondered if the little tree survived our love.

ILL. It did, I –

CLAIRE ZACHANASSIAN (*continued from above*). Other
things didn't –

ILL (*continued from above*). – I just can't pinpoint where it is.

CLAIRE ZACHANASSIAN (*continued from above*). – and
I wondered about you, naturally, everywhere I've been, and
I've been in some remarkable places – the whorehouse in
Hamburg, for instance, where Zachanassian found me, and
paid for me, and fell for me, and married and enriched me,
and died after the war, old beyond his years, which exceeded
mine by several decades. There's a Hamburg disinfectant
they used on the sheets and towels and floors, it smelled like
Slurry to me, a little like what they'd wash out my father's
shithouses with, back then, and so it reminded me of you.

You and I made love in the public toilets if it was raining too hard for the woods, after Peterson's barn filled with rats, because we had no choice, we had to. Time and the world swallowed you up, Alfred, my first lover, my first true love, and this forest, and this town, and I can't forget you.

ILL. We need you, Clara.

CLAIRE ZACHANASSIAN. I know.

ILL. *I* need you.

CLAIRE ZACHANASSIAN. Maybe that's so.

ILL. More than you know.

CLAIRE ZACHANASSIAN. How much more?

ILL. I... I'm not sure I –

CLAIRE ZACHANASSIAN. How much?

How much, Alfred?

How much do you need?

ILL. The town? Millions.

CLAIRE ZACHANASSIAN. Chump change.

ILL. Many millions.

CLAIRE ZACHANASSIAN. Many chumps.

ILL. Help us, Clara? Lift us up? Give us a future?

CLAIRE ZACHANASSIAN. The town?

Absolutely.

(*Calling up to the* GUYS.) Doby! Roby! Rub-a-dub-dub!

The two GUYS *bring the sedan chair.* CLAIRE ZACHANASSIAN *gets in.*

(*To* ILL.) Nice, huh? It's from the Pinacoteca Ambrosiana in Milan, a present to me from Pius XII. It carried Lucrezia Borgia to her assignations with Bembo. They sang madrigals to one another, contrapuntally.

As DOBY *and* ROBY *raise the chair,* ILL *grabs* CLAIRE ZACHANASSIAN*'s hand and kisses it, passionately.*

ILL. Perfect and cold as it always was.

CLAIRE ZACHANASSIAN. More perfect now. Colder. See?

She twists her wrist and pulls back her arm; her hand comes off. ILL *holds it a moment, then screams and drops it.* ROBY *and* DOBY *crack up.* DOBY *bends to retrieve it, holding the sedan chair perfectly level with just one arm. He returns it to its owner.*

The Swiss made it for me from a Chinese design, Wu Dai Shi Guo Dynasty.

ILL. Jesus Christ, are you totally fake?

CLAIRE ZACHANASSIAN. Aren't we all? (*Screwing the hand back in place.*) My plane crashed in the Hindu Kush. I got out, my hand didn't.

(*Tosses her cigar to the ground.*) Roby! Extinguish! Doby! A stogie!

ROBY *grinds the stub into the earth with his boot, while* DOBY *fetches another cigar from his jeans.* CLAIRE ZACHANASSIAN *lights up, tosses the match into the needles beneath her, and off they go.*

ILL *puts out the fire she's started and watches them go, then follows them. He stops suddenly by a tree. He looks at it, then calls after* CLAIRE ZACHANASSIAN:

ILL. Look! Here it is! A and C! It's Alfred and Clara, it's, it's us!

He realizes they're not turning back. He looks at the carving in the tree, touches it.

(*Softly.*) The tree didn't die. Neither did you. Or me. Nobody died, right? And wounds fade away, Claire, mostly, and when all's said and done, what's left behind is love. (*Looking at the carving on the tree.*) The memory of love.

He pursues.

Scene Three

The Grand Ballroom of the Lake Erie Hotel, that night. Once truly grand, the ballroom's grimy disrepair has been covered up with decorations for tonight's banquet as much as Slurry's dire financial straits allow, which is to say it's depressingly unfestive. The SLURRIANS *sit at tables, feasting.* MAYOR HERCKHEIMER *and his wife,* EDELTRUD HERCKHEIMER, REVEREND MESSING, MISS COVINGTON, DR NUTLING, ILL *and his wife,* MATTIE ILL, *are on a raised dais, above which the 'WELCOME CLAIRIE!!!' banner from the train station is now suspended.* CLAIRE ZACHANASSIAN *is seated at the center of the table; the chair next to her, unoccupied, is for* HUSBAND #7.

The AFTER-SCHOOL TUMBLERS *are concluding a demonstration of their skills before the dais. When they're done, everyone in the hall applauds, except for* CLAIRE ZACHANASSIAN.

MAYOR HERCKHEIMER. Thank you, thank you, After-School Tumblers, for that marvelous postprandial entertainment! Nothing aids digestion so well as watching young people in a gymnastics display. I hope our guest of honor found their exertions salubrious.

CLAIRE ZACHANASSIAN. Indeed she does. Who doesn't relish the chance to watch the unforgivable young learn to endure torture? Look at them, panting; look at the muscles they're developing. Think how efficiently any one of them could choke the wind from some malefactor's throat. (*To the* TUMBLERS.) Any of you ever tried strangling?

EDELTRUD HERCKHEIMER. Mrs Zachanassian!

CLAIRE ZACHANASSIAN (*peering through her monocle*). It's Edeltrud Dummermut, isn't it? Of course you married the mayor, you always liked bossing the rest of us around. You look like you swallowed a hatbox, Trudie, or is that a goiter? (*To the* TUMBLERS.) Any of you think you could wrap your hands around a neck that fat?

MAYOR *and* EDELTRUD HERCKHEIMER. Mrs
Zachanassian!!!

ILL. You always laughed at horror, Clara. I loved that about
you.

MATTIE. She's being morbid, and and tasteless! I'm sorry, Mrs
Zachanassian, but – They're children!

REVEREND MESSING. Let's send them back to their parents'
tables, and –

MATTIE (*continued from above*). She oughtn't to tell them to
murder people, that's not –

CLAIRE ZACHANASSIAN. Mattie Ill, née Grimke. You were
so roly-poly, once upon a time. You've gone as gaunt as
bossie Edeltrud's ballooned. You look like you're being fed
some gradual poison. Does marriage not agree with you?

REVEREND MESSING. Shall we commence the ceremonial
portion of the evening?

MAYOR HERCKHEIMER. We're waiting for Mrs
Zachanassian's husband.

CLAIRE ZACHANASSIAN. Oh don't wait for Moby. I divorced
him earlier this evening – I forgot to let him know! And he
hates surprises, like stupid people do.

REVEREND MESSING. You seemed such a happy couple.

CLAIRE ZACHANASSIAN. It was after visiting the church,
where I used to go when I was a girl to sit under that fresco
of the world consumed by fire and blood, contemplating
suicide, or murder, or marriage – (*To* MATTIE.) Teenagers
are so dramatic, aren't they, Millie? I dreamed of marrying in
that church. And now I shall!

ILL. It's Mattie not –

MATTIE. Who are you going to marry?

CLAIRE ZACHANASSIAN (*calling out*). Boby! Who am
I marrying?

BOBY. French absurdist playwright.

CLAIRE ZACHANASSIAN. A *playwright*? A *frog* playwright?! NO! I ordered an Italian neo-realist film director!

BOBY (*offstage*). I'll call the procurers.

CLAIRE ZACHANASSIAN. They're slipping!! Look at #7. I mean! What is *that*? (*To* MAYOR HERCKHEIMER.) The wedding's tomorrow morning. Which is why I'm anxious to get business taken care of tonight.

The hall is instantly aflame with whispered repetition of 'business'. ILL *grins at* MAYOR HERCKHEIMER, *who rises, clears his throat and taps the side of his wine glass with a spoon.*

MAYOR HERCKHEIMER. Then let us neither shilly nor shally nor tardily tarry, shall we?

He smiles, waiting for the laugh, but there's only hushed, expectant silence.

My dear dear *dear* Mrs Zachanassian, little Clairie Mucker, first and best daughter of Slurry, first in the hearts of your fellow Slurrians: Welcome home, Clairie!

As the hall erupts in cheers, MAYOR HERCKHEIMER *pulls a thick sheaf of folded pages from his inner breast pocket: His speech, handwritten and so heavily worked-over that right away he has trouble reading it.*

We remember you like you only left yesterday, left to seek your fortune in the great wide expanse out beyond the Slurry town limits. Since you've returned it's like not a day has passed since last your infectious joy and your irrepressible mischievous… joy and your effervescent humor brightened our lives with your unpredictable originality, your, your love of forestry and, and – let's not forget how once when you were in high school, you gave a hungry old lady some potatoes! Mrs Zachanassian, how can we say that we deserve you?

CLAIRE ZACHANASSIAN. Succinctly!

MAYOR HERCKHEIMER. Sorry, my speech, it's so scribbled-over it's – Aaah, to hell with it! (*Throws the pages away.*) You want succinct? Good people! I raise my glass –

He does this, and all others except CLAIRE ZACHANASSIAN *raise their glasses;* MATTIE *requires a little encouragement from* ILL.

To Claire Zachanassian née Mucker, citizeness of Slurry and of the great wide world: Long life! Long life and happiness! Hip hip –

The room responds with a mighty 'Hooray' followed by prolonged cheering, the AFTER-SCHOOL TUMBLERS *flipping about and the* MIXED-RACE CHOIR *bursting into 'On the Sunny Side of the Street'.*

CLAIRE ZACHANASSIAN *watches this for a moment, then rises. The room is instantly quiet.*

CLAIRE ZACHANASSIAN. Wow. Whodathunkit? All for me, lost little me. The potatoes – (*To* ILL.) Freddy, you told them about the potatoes, I bet you didn't mention I swiped them from the grocery and swapped them for one afternoon in the old hag's bed, I wanted to do it with him in a real bed, just once, to see what it was like. It was nice. (*To* ILL.) Wasn't it, Ill?

ILL. Oh! *Yeah!* That was beyond – (*Remembers* MATTIE, *blushes, looks down at his flatware.*)

CLAIRE ZACHANASSIAN. I think that's when you got me pregnant. Doesn't matter. What matters, my good people, is what's done, and what we do. And what can and cannot be undone.

NOW: Here's what I intend to do:

I come prepared to give Slurry a present of one billion dollars.

Astounded silence.

Five hundred million to replenish the town's coffers. Five hundred million to be divided equally among you.

More astounded silence, then WILD JUBILATION!
Cheering! Weeping! Tumbling! The MIXED-RACE CHOIR
sings 'Honey in the Honeycomb'. ILL *rushes to* CLAIRE
ZACHANASSIAN's *side and kisses her on the mouth, or*
tries to; she is as rigid and unyielding as stone. ILL *turns*
immediately and kisses MATTIE, *who isn't especially*
pleased by his attention. He turns to the CROWD *and roars:*

ILL. She's, she's good as gold, heart of gold, golden-souled,
she's my Clara, when all's said and done she said and did
what she had to do, for us, for –

CLAIRE ZACHANASSIAN. Pause.

One condition:

Silence.

I'm giving you the billion, and the billion buys me justice.

MAYOR HERCKHEIMER. You… You want to buy justice?

CLAIRE ZACHANASSIAN. A billion should do it.

MAYOR HERCKHEIMER. But justice, it, it isn't for sale. Is it?

CLAIRE ZACHANASSIAN. I've bought it before.

Boby. Here.

BOBY *stands before the dais, removes his dark glasses and*
stares at the room.

BOBY. Anybody know me? It's been years.

Murmuring among the SLURRIANS, *then:*

MISS COVINGTON. You're… Is it Judge Huffer? But, but you
moved to Albany, years and years ago, you –

BOBY. Appointed to the State Supreme Court, that's correct,
forty-five years ago, Associate Justice till Brandeis stepped
up to the U.S. Supreme Court and I was appointed to his
seat, State Supreme Court Chief Justice Huffer then, which is
where I was when Mrs Zachanassian approached me with an
offer of employment as her butler. I was a jurist of
distinction, and a scholar, too, I was almost done with the

third revision of my classic textbook, *Amortization, Depreciation and Depletion Laws*. I thought she was mad, but the salary she proposed was so fantastic –

CLAIRE ZACHANASSIAN. Wrap it up, Boby.

BOBY. Mrs Zachanassian is willing to pay one billion dollars in cold hard cash and she wants her money to buy her justice. In other words: Mrs Zachanassian is willing to pay one billion dollars cash on the barrel and she wants her money to buy her justice.

MAYOR HERCKHEIMER. But, but still, still I –

MISS COVINGTON. Mrs Zachanassian, you didn't buy justice, you bought *a* justice; the indefinite article transforms the noun from an abstract concept into a man of flesh and blood, the frail mortal who stands before us. That men, *some* men, to use a determiner, some men can be bought, and women too, as you are aware, dear lady, that isn't news, but how can one buy an abstraction?

CLAIRE ZACHANASSIAN. Interesting question. Most likely: start with the specific, proceed to the general. Boby?

BOBY. Mr Ill?

ILL. What?

BOBY. Join me, please.

ILL. Why?

BOBY. Please.

ILL *looks at* CLAIRE ZACHANASSIAN, *who is not looking at him. He laughs, looks around. Everyone else is looking at him but no one else is laughing. He shrugs and strides, blustery-tough, to* BOBY'*s side.*

ILL. Present and accounted for, reporting for duty, at your service and so on.

BOBY. In 1910 an affiliation proceeding was brought to my court, here in Slurry, a paternity suit, instituted by the unwed mother, Claire Mucker, a minor, acting *in loco parentis* because her parents were deceased, against you, Alfred Ill. You denied paternity. Under oath.

He looks at ILL, *waiting for a response.* ILL *doesn't respond. Then:*

ILL (*angry*). So?!

Then a look in CLAIRE ZACHANASSIAN's *direction, crumbling a bit.*

I, maybe I should'nt've, but, that was, I was a kid myself, what was I, eighteen? Nineteen? Who isn't a jerk at that age?

BOBY. You brought two witnesses.

ILL. I did?

BOBY (*calling off*). Doby, Roby, bring Koby and Loby.

DOBY *leads* KOBY *and* LOBY *in, both grinning.* ROBY *follows with his guitar slung on his back.*

KOBY. We smell food.

LOBY. Smells good!

KOBY. Barbecue chicken!

LOBY. Coleslaw!

BOBY. Mr Ill? Know who they are?

ILL *doesn't answer.*

(*To* KOBY *and* LOBY.) Tell him.

KOBY *and* LOBY (*their soft-shoe routine*). We're Koby and Loby! Loby and Koby! Nobody Anybody! Doughbody Antibody!

ILL. I don't know who these clowns are, they're, they're… entertainers, or –

KOBY. We know you. We did, before –

LOBY. We were altered.

KOBY. At the altar.

LOBY. Translated. With a knife.

BOBY. Who were you?

> *Beat.* KOBY *and* LOBY *stand there, grinning, but the grins have hardened.*

> Who were you?

KOBY. Virgil Duckworth.

LOBY. Perch. Walter Perch.

BOBY. Mr Ill? Ring any –

ILL. That's, that's bullshit, that's not – (*To* KOBY *and* LOBY.) You're lying, you're not –

BOBY. Koby and Loby, does Mr Ill look familiar to you?

KOBY. He looks like night without light looks, Mr Boby.

LOBY. We're blinded and blind.

BOBY. What about his voice?

LOBY. Oh sure, his voice –

KOBY. Deeper, and –

LOBY. – gruffer, Chief Justice Huffer, but –

KOBY. – it's Freddy alright.

LOBY. It's Ill.

KOBY *and* LOBY. Alfred Ill.

BOBY. Good. And when you were before me in my court in 1910, what was your testimony, under oath?

KOBY. We swore we'd fucked Clairie, that we'd fucked her and fucked her.

LOBY. Swore we knew others who'd fucked Clairie Mucker.

BOBY. Was that true?

LOBY. We perjured ourselves.

KOBY. We lied and lied!

BOBY. Why?

KOBY. For a laugh.

LOBY. For a lark.

KOBY. For the beers Freddy promised.

CLAIRE ZACHANASSIAN. And what happened then?

LOBY. You hunted us down.

KOBY. She hunted us down! She's Artemis.

KOBY *and* LOBY. Artemis!

LOBY. Pitiless huntress!

KOBY. Walt went to Canada.

LOBY. Gill fled to Mexico.

CLAIRE ZACHANASSIAN. And then? What then?

KOBY. You castrated us.

LOBY. You blinded us.

KOBY. You made us your chorus.

BOBY. Plaintiff, is this true?

    CLAIRE ZACHANASSIAN *rises*.

And the plaintiff's newborn baby?

    CLAIRE ZACHANASSIAN *doesn't respond*.

You were nine months pregnant when you appeared before my bench, seeking justice. After I ruled against you on the evidence presented, you must have given birth.

CLAIRE ZACHANASSIAN. Immediately after. My anguish... evicted her.

BOBY. And what happened to her mother.

CLAIRE ZACHANASSIAN. I became a whore.

BOBY. Why?

CLAIRE ZACHANASSIAN. The finding of the court.

BOBY. And your child?

CLAIRE ZACHANASSIAN. One year old. A cold released her. Erased her.

BOBY. An old story now. And now, Claire Zachanassian, née Mucker of Slurry? What is it you want?

CLAIRE ZACHANASSIAN. Justice.

One billion dollars for the town of Slurry, if someone kills Alfred Ill.

Dead silence.

Then MATTIE *screams, a loud, long scream.*

Silence again. Then:

ILL. Clara. Life's terrible but it goes on, on and on. And I'm still Alfred, and you're still –

CLAIRE ZACHANASSIAN. Still. Exactly. I'm still. I'm still. The roses are still blooming, the stream is still flowing, the trout are still swimming, the clouds are still rolling by, time hurries past but you're still what you were and I'm still what you made me, time hurries past us but nothing passes or changes, we wizen, we shrivel, bits get cut off and tossed out like table scraps, we tarnish and scar but we're still who we were, who we were's what we are. You've kissed me, Alfred, twice today; you wanted those kisses to brush the years away. But that's unnecessary; *Time only ever stands still.* And I still want justice. I paid plenty for the wrong you did, now I've the means – one billion dollars to set things right. One billion for your blood.

A beat. No one moves. Then:

MAYOR HERCKHEIMER. Mrs Zachanassian, we're not in Europe, where you've lived for so long, not in Switzerland, where you sheltered for the war. No. We're in America. *You're* in America, Mrs Zachanassian, you're in the town of Slurry, in Chautauqua County, in Western New York State, on the shore of Lake Erie, in the United States of America, and in the name of all of the above, in the name of humanity itself, Mrs Zachanassian, in my official capacity as mayor, elected by these good people here:

There's no shame in poverty. We don't want blood money. Your offer is rejected, flat-out.

Tremendous applause which goes on until it dies, during which CLAIRE ZACHANASSIAN *sits. When the room once more is silent:*

CLAIRE ZACHANASSIAN. I'll wait.

ROBY *plays his guitar.*

End of Act One.

ACT TWO

Scene One

ILL*'s general store. A large window looking out on a street of mostly empty shops with 'FOR SALE' and 'FOR LEASE' signs in their windows. On* ILL*'s window, painted with copper paint now turned green, 'ILL'S GENERAL STORE'. Inside, an old wooden counter, heavily scarred, stretched in front of tall shelves spottily stocked with merchandise, dusty, unappealing.* ANNALISE ILL, ILL*'s sixteen-year-old daughter, wearing an apron and a dustcap, is sweeping the floor.* ZACHARY ILL, ILL*'s eighteen-year-old son, is practicing rolling a cigarette.*

ILL *is behind the counter in his shopkeeper's apron. He's sorting through bills. He looks up as* DOBY *and* ROBY *saunter insolently past his window,* ROBY *strumming his guitar,* DOBY *carrying a large funeral wreath, crossed with a ribbon on which 'ETERNAL IN OUR MEMORY' is boldly printed.* DOBY *looks into the store and winks at* ILL*; then the pair and the wreath are gone.*

ILL. That's the second one today.

(*Looks at his bills. Then:*) They're marching them past the store to frighten me.

ZACHARY. That coffin that came with her? It's got a whole hotel room, all to itself, and that's where the wreaths go. It's open to the public.

ILL. Fucking hell.

ZACHARY. No one's going in to look. I mean, some are, but... Don't be scared, Pop.

ILL. I'm not! Who says I'm –

ZACHARY. You were...

ILL. What?

ZACHARY. Yesterday you sorta hid out upstairs. Seemed that way, the whole day, we didn't even see you at supper.

ILL (*nodding, looking down at the bills*). I didn't have much of an appetite.

ZACHARY. She's trying to shake us up, but. Nobody's shaken, Pop. The whole town's with you.

ILL. It's good people, this town.

ZACHARY. Screw her and her thugs.

ILL (*fondly*). Watch your mouth.

ZACHARY. Screw her and her billion.

ILL (*to* ANNALISE). Where's your mother?

ANNALISE *doesn't look up or stop sweeping.*

ZACHARY (*to* ANNALISE). He asked you a question.

ILL. It's alright, leave her be.

(*To* ANNALISE.) You're disappointed in me. At what I did. You're right to be. I'm, I'm disappointed in myself. You kids, you're better than I was, I gave you more, much more than I ever got. I grew up lawless, thought I was some kind of tough, thought I had to be. I made sure you kids got what I didn't. I've been a good provider, haven't I been?

ZACHARY. Sure, Pop. You did what you could.

ILL. Hey, watch it with the past tense. I'm still doing!

(*To* ANNALISE.) Go ask your mom if she wants breakfast. I'm cooking. Eggs and canned hash!

ZACHARY *tucks his rolled cigarette behind his ear and starts for the door.*

Where are you going? I said I'm cooking –

ZACHARY. The road crew on the Milestrip Highway needs temporaries, I'm gonna fill in.

ILL. That's hard labor, that's for prisoners, for negroes and laid-off whites, not for people like us. When did you decide this?

ZACHARY. Since you've been shuffling and reshuffling those bills every morning.

ILL. I been shuffling bills since you were in diapers. Why now? Never mind, I –

ZACHARY. We don't need the money, Pop?

ILL. Never mind I said.

ANNALISE (*to ZACHARY, taking off her apron and cap*). Hang on a minute, I'll walk out with you.

ILL. Now I know you're not thinking of road work, little girl.

ANNALISE. If you wait by the library, sometimes ladies come by, for girls who do housework.

ILL. My daughter is not – You're not a maid! Does your mother know that you –

ANNALISE. I want to help, Daddy. I know how to sweep.

ILL (*very moved*). Your mother and me, we raised two fine children.

ZACHARY. We're broke.

MR HOFBAUER, *a local butcher, enters the store*.

ANNALISE. It's temporary.

The KIDS *leave*.

ILL. Look at those kids. Aren't they too much.

MR HOFBAUER. Two days ago you said they was bums.

ILL. I never – I said *he* was a bum. And, and I said she was a brat. Wrong, as usual. I'm always wrong about –

MR HOFBAUER. Pack of cigarettes.

ILL (*reaching on a shelf for a pack of cigarettes*). Sure thing.

MR HOFBAUER. Don't give me them Camels, I want Kents!

ILL. You always get Camels.

MR HOFBAUER. None of that unfiltered shit, not anymore, not for me. Gimme a pack with micronite filters!

ILL. Kents are twice as expensive as –

MR HOFBAUER. House account.

ILL. You don't have a –

MR HOFBAUER. I'd like to start a house account.

ILL (*a beat, then:*). You're one of my oldest customers, Hofbauer, and what have we got if we can't trust one another, at a time like this? Here.

ILL *hands* MR HOFBAUER *a packet of Kents. Then, as* ILL *finds a new notebook on the shelves, opens it, and enters* MR HOFBAUER*'s purchase in it,* KOBY *and* LOBY *enter the store, wearing* HUSBAND #7*'s fishing gear, holding hands, each with a pole in the other hand, grinning.*

KOBY. Morning, Freddy!

LOBY. We're off to the brook!

KOBY. Off to catch trout! Wanna come?!

ILL *rushes around the counter, charging at them.*

ILL (*roaring*). OUT! OUT OF MY STORE! WHOEVER OR *WHAT*EVER YOU ARE!!

LOBY (*smiling, not budging*). We need a pretty kettle to put the fishes in.

KOBY. Do you have a pretty kettle to –

ILL. OUT!!! DOES THIS LOOK LIKE A CIRCUS TENT?!

KOBY *and* LOBY *laugh and leave, saying as they go:*

KOBY. How would we know what it looks like, Fred?

LOBY. She took our looking, Fred, she took our eyes.

KOBY *and* LOBY (*singing as they go*). We're Koby and Loby, you cannot ignore us, the Old Lady's chorus, in Sheol she owns us…

ILL *slams the door behind them.*

MR HOFBAUER. Eunuchs, are they?

ILL. She's trying to rattle me.

MR HOFBAUER. The flyreel and the waders and all that get-up, that was her husband's.

ILL (*going back behind the counter, recording* MR HOFBAUER's *account*). Ex-husband.

MR HOFBAUER. That's right, her ex- . Shipped out on the Zephyr. The new husband's a Frenchy, I heard him, at the wedding. You wasn't there.

ILL. Not interested.

MR HOFBAUER. I bet. Newspaper people were practically parachuting in! Movie stars and a delegation of Senators and the, whatsisname, the Aga Khan! I didn't see him, but they say he was there! The Catholic church is so shiny now you'd never know it! That sign-painter fella, he touched up the fresco for her. And a Champagne fountain!

Two townswomen, MRS BALK *and* MRS CREEKY, *enter, carrying empty milk cans.*

And snails!

MRS BALK. Naturally *you* went, Hofbauer, always harking to free liquor's siren call.

The two WOMEN *put their cans on the counter.*

MRS BALK *and* MRS CREEKY. Milk, Mr Ill.

ILL. Milk it is, ladies.

He takes two bottles of skim milk from a shelf.

MRS CREEKY. Not skim. Whole milk for me.

MRS BALK. A quart of whole for me, and one half-and-half.

ILL. Pricey.

MRS BALK. Sometimes a body needs the fortification of fat. A pound of butter too.

MR HOFBAUER. The snails she served was swimming in garlic butter.

MRS CREEKY. Butter for me too, five pounds of flour, *and!* I'll have a look at that electric iron in the window.

ILL. No kidding? Some rich uncle die?

The two WOMEN *look at each other, then:*

MRS BALK. Can we open a tab? Like a, a…?

MRS CREEKY. Charge account. We're good for it, I think you know that.

ILL. Yeah, I know you're… It's not how we usually do things but… It'd be unseemly to say no, I guess, so… Sure. All for one, one for all.

MRS BALK. And a Whitman's Sampler.

MRS CREEKY. No, the Valentine chocolates with the brandied cherry centers!

MRS BALK. We'll eat a few of them while you ready our order.

MRS CREEKY. I woke up this morning, Ill, thinking of that woman –

MRS BALK. That terrible woman.

MRS CREEKY. – and how she set you up, set all of us up, playing on our great need for – You shouldn't've oughta behaved that way, Ill.

MRS BALK. Nor she shouldn't've oughta let you. But that's another story.

MRS CREEKY. That said, I woke up this morning with my heart full of sorrow for you, for all of us, but with that sorrow, something was there I haven't felt for a while, I'll admit it: Neighborly affection.

ILL. I'll get the chocolates and the iron.

ILL *takes a fancy box of chocolates shaped like a heart from a shelf and gives it to* MRS CREEKY. *He goes to the window next to remove an electric iron from the display. He blows the dust off, takes off the price tag and, seeing it's low, slips it in his pocket. Another customer,* MR EMERSON, *enters.*

Days pass with that door opening only for kids and moochers! All a sudden, I'm busy!

MR EMERSON. We want to show you our support, Al old pal.

ILL. Al?

MR EMERSON. It's a nickname I made up this morning!

MRS CREEKY. Have a brandied cherry chocolate, Mr Emerson?

MR EMERSON. Is it Valentine's Day?!

He takes a chocolate.

MRS CREEKY (*over the above*). A billion dollars'd be swell but okay, alright, we just have to help one another, and trust one another, stay in step, be flexible, and we'll be fine.

And just waking up feeling that way, it's enough to make the world seem richer and more abundant.

MRS BALK. There's deep wells of affection in Slurry for you, Al. You're one of ours. Rest assured.

MR EMERSON. Dead sure. Dead sure.

MRS CREEKY. There's no price you can put on a single human life. That's certain.

MR EMERSON. Dead sure. Dead –

ILL. Please stop saying that.

MR EMERSON. A bottle of beer, if you please. No, make that whiskey.

ILL. You can't afford whiskey. Your liver can't afford it either.

MR HOFBAUER. They must've invented bubbly just to wash down snails with! She-Devil she may be, but she sure throws a shindig!

MR EMERSON. Wasn't it lovely? And gimme that special Dutch tobacco that smells like cookies baking on Christmas morning.

MRS CREEKY. Ooh, I'll take some for my husband's pipe!

ILL. It's seven bucks a pouch!

MR EMERSON. Charge it to my account.

MRS CREEKY. Ditto.

ILL, *looking troubled, places the iron on the counter, gets two packets of pipe tobacco from a shelf, and under the counter, he retrieves a very dusty bottle of whiskey.* MR EMERSON *takes the bottle, pockets one of the tobacco pouches, and as he's walking towards the door he rubs the dust off the label, inspecting it.*

ILL (*troubled*). Okay, I guess… you pay me Monday with your relief check, Emerson?

MR EMERSON, *ignoring him, is opening the door when* ILL *stops him by yelling:*

HALT! HANG ON!

ILL *runs around the counter and up to* MR EMERSON. *He pulls up one of* MR EMERSON's *pants legs.*

Sonofabitch! Those shoes!

MR EMERSON. Nice, huh?

ILL. They're brand new! I heard 'em squeaking! You've been wearing the same old loafers since –

Struck by a sudden thought, he wheels around to MR HOFBAUER, *who is smoking a Kent.*

Stick out your foot, Hofbauer.

MR HOFBAUER. My what?

ILL. Your foot, your foot, your goddamned –

MR HOFBAUER *complies*.

Goddamn it. Brand new. Same as Emerson.

MR HOFBAUER. I got 'em for the wedding. I don't see how it's none of your –

ILL *turns to the two* WOMEN*; sheepishly they withdraw their new-shoe-shod feet from his glare*.

ILL (*to* MRS CREEKY). Your husband hasn't worked a day in two years. You got five kids. *Patent leather?!*

MRS CREEKY. On credit. Buchbinder and Quelt's.

ILL (*a beat, then:*). How, how many stores offering credit? Since yesterday?

MRS BALK. Pretty much every store. When one does, the others have to, right? It's, it's common sense is all, to say nothing of common courtesy. You don't need to make us feel like we stole 'em.

MRS CREEKY. It's economics, Creeky says, what we're seeing is an economic stimulus of some kind or –

ILL. You can't stimulate what's not there! How can you stimulate… gutted-out savings accounts and old unpaid bills?!

MR HOFBAUER. Like you know! Criticizing others for what you're doing yourself.

ILL. I'm not doing anything! And I wasn't criticizing, but, but this is, it's worrisome, it's –

MR EMERSON (*over the above*). That's right, Al. You're extending credit, so why shouldn't the next fella?

ILL. But, but look here, man, you can't just buy and not – How will you pay your debts?

He stares at them, panic rising. They stare back, puzzled.

MR HOFBAUER. Can't say I care much for your tone, Al.

ILL. Oh my God. Oh my God. The whole town's out… buying stuff on time. Isn't it.

MRS BALK. You don't want to extend me a line of credit, just say as much.

MRS CREEKY. We can go elsewhere.

ILL suddenly feels faint, sick to his stomach, terrified. He runs to the door behind the counter, repeating to himself as he goes:

ILL. How will you pay what you owe? Any of you? Are you asking yourselves that? You have to ask that, because, because somehow you'll have to pay your bills.

First Interstitial

On a balcony of the Lake Eerie Hotel, CLAIRE ZACHANASSIAN *watches as, in the street below,* ILL *storms, indignant, furious, wary, from the shop to the police station.* BELSHA *is painting a wedding portrait.* CLAIRE ZACHANASSIAN *is dressed like an Ancient Greek statue, white silk chiton and shawl, a broad-brimmed, conical straw hat on her head or behind her or at her side.* HUSBAND #8, *a French absurdist playwright, glum, still in his morning suit from the wedding, sits in a chair next to where* CLAIRE ZACHANASSIAN'*s standing.* BOBY *stands nearby.*

CLAIRE ZACHANASSIAN (*pointing to the street below*). And off he goes. Motion, and – (*Gesturing to herself.*) Stillness. Motion is narrative, time becoming story becoming history. Stillness is… a whole other thing.

BELSHA. Stillness is critical if the subject wants a decent resemblance. So please keep your head still. And stop moving your lips.

CLAIRE ZACHANASSIAN. The subject is paying for the portrait, therefore the subject will move whatso'er she likes. My lips giving you a problem?

BELSHA. Not in the least. (*Seductively*.) They're fascinating.

CLAIRE ZACHANASSIAN (*returning the seductive tone*). Memorable, or so I'm told.

BELSHA. Unforgettable.

CLAIRE ZACHANASSIAN. Don't overdo it.

HUSBAND #8. *Mais pourquoi ne puis-je pas être dans cette peinture?* Whhy you tell ziss man not to paint me?

CLAIRE ZACHANASSIAN. You won't last long enough for the oil to dry. *Ars longa, matrimonium brevis*. Or would it be matrimonium brev*i*?

HUSBAND #8. Zen eff I am so *comment-dit-on… disponible*, whhy you insist zat I muss pose wiss you?!

CLAIRE ZACHANASSIAN. In years to come, when I look at the painting, if I ever do, the vacancy behind me will remind me not of you but of how much I enjoyed expunging you. (*To* BELSHA.) I ask for an Italian neo-realist film director; they send a French absurdist playwright. People think because you're rich you get exactly what you want. (*To* BOBY.) Have you found my leg?

BOBY. Not yet.

CLAIRE ZACHANASSIAN. Moby took it, of course, his petty revenge, my fault for hurling it at his tiny head as he fled out the door. Bring me one of the spares – the Dresden china leg – (*To* BELSHA.) Painted all over with sweet little boys flying kites.

HUSBAND #8 (*with Gallic disgust*). *Il est épouvantable!*

CLAIRE ZACHANASSIAN (*to* HUSBAND #8). Oh just GO! I hate French theater, and absurdism makes it worse! You're fooling no one, you frogs: the giddy relief with which you opened wide for the Nazis was scandalous, and now not all your cutesy-wootsy clouds of baby-talk can hide what it revealed: you're cheap and you like it rough! Give me realism, show me something *real*, if anything really is – by 'real' I suppose I mean POTENT, which you, *chéri, ain't.* Boby!! Fetch the leg. And please have this, this marginalia transported back to Paris.

HUSBAND #8. *Madame, vous êtes une infâme putain.*

CLAIRE ZACHANASSIAN. *Et pourtant, vous êtes celui qui vendu sa chatte pour un salaire de graisse.*

BOBY. *Monsieur?*

HUSBAND #8 *stalks off the balcony.* BOBY *follows him.* BELSHA *paints.* CLAIRE ZACHANASSIAN *is absolutely still, like a statue.*

BELSHA. That's why the toga, to cover up your missing leg?

CLAIRE ZACHANASSIAN. It's a chiton, not a toga. My mobility's been diminishing, limb by limb. I don't miss it in the least. The truth's in the attic and needs no legs. Stillness is truth; motion is the lie. (*Calling after* BOBY.) BOBY!!! I'm feeling naked without my leg!!

Scene Two

The Slurry police station. PERCY *sits on a bench in his father's police uniform, which doesn't fit well, playing with a pair of handcuffs.* CHIEF MUNDZUK *is behind the station desk in civilian's clothing, loading ammo into an array of rifles and revolvers laid out on the desk, next to a half-drained bottle of wine and a plate of cheese and crackers. There's a radio on which* The Merry Widow *is playing.* ILL *enters and addresses* CHIEF MUNDZUK.

ILL. Mundzuk, I want to file a complaint against –

CHIEF MUNDZUK (*not looking up from his gun-loading, indicating* PERCY). Talk to him. I don't work here anymore.

ILL. Him?! He's a kid! He's your –

CHIEF MUNDZUK. Mayor hired him.

ILL. And you're working for Clara – for Zachanassian now.

CHIEF MUNDZUK. Well, sort of. Everyone's so set against her, her offer of the billion bucks for… You know. I'm… confused about the ethics. Of working for her. Meantime, you got a complaint, talk to the kid. I mean, talk to Officer Mundzuk.

ILL (*to* PERCY). I want to bring charges against Claire Zachanassian.

PERCY. For what?

ILL. You were there! Both of you! She's trying to have me killed!

PERCY. Yeah. Uh, I don't know. I don't think she meant that.

ILL. I don't care what you think! You're not old enough to drink beer! (*To* CHIEF MUNDZUK.) This is nuts, put on your goddamned uniform and arrest her!

CHIEF MUNDZUK. The kid's right, Ill.

ILL. He's wrong! I know her!

CHIEF MUNDZUK. I know you know her. The whole town knows how well you –

PERCY *giggles*.

PERCY. You said she had a weird sense of humor. When she told the tumblers to learn how to strangle people, you said that she was –

ILL. That was before I realized she was – She was recruiting assassins, you moron!!

CHIEF MUNDZUK. Out in the open for all the world to see.

ILL. She, she thinks her money will – She's so rich she thinks she can get away with –

CHIEF MUNDZUK. Yeah, and about that. Calm yourself a little, Mr Ill, and ask yourself: One billion dollars? Just to kill a guy like you? Doesn't that seem a little, I dunno, inflated?

PERCY. Hey yeah, that's true!

CHIEF MUNDZUK. Ask around down by the lakefront, they got guys there'd do her that service for five hundred bucks no questions asked. The old lady, she doesn't seem stupid to me. Eccentric enough but not a cuckoo –

ILL. She isn't crazy, or stupid. She's a, a monster! She's evil!

PERCY. *She* didn't leave *you* holding a bastard on your lonesome, that was *you* did that, and don't say you was young, I'm younger'n you were back then, and I know how low it is, what you done. In fact, anyone should be arrested, if you ask me, it ain't Mrs Z. And if you ask me again for what you just now asked me to do, I might consider you a public nuisance, and, anyhow, just don't. Okay?

CHIEF MUNDZUK *turns up the radio.*

CHIEF MUNDZUK. I love this part. (*To* ILL.) *The Merry Widow.*

ILL. When did you get a radio?

CHIEF MUNDZUK. Yesterday. None of your –

ILL. Let me see your feet!

CHIEF MUNDZUK. Get lost!

ILL. And since when do you drink wine?

CHIEF MUNDZUK. I'm not on duty.

CHIEF MUNDZUK *resumes loading a gun.* ILL *freezes, then:*

ILL. Should you be doing that while you're drinking?

CHIEF MUNDZUK. The old lady's panther escaped.

PERCY. It's super-dangerous.

CHIEF MUNDZUK. We have to hunt it down.

PERCY. Kill it. The whole town's arming up.

ILL. You're, you're not hunting panthers.

CHIEF MUNDZUK (*grins*). No?

ILL. You're gonna hunt –

You have a gold tooth.

CHIEF MUNDZUK *stops grinning*.

I saw it! You have a new gold tooth in your –

CHIEF MUNDZUK. It's *my* mouth. I paid for it.

ILL. *How?! How did you –*

CHIEF MUNDZUK. You're paranoid.

(*Picks up a gun.*) I got to get these oiled and loaded and handed out.

PERCY. We got to adjust the sights.

CHIEF MUNDZUK *points a gun at* ILL, *and then looks down the sight, fiddling with it*.

CHIEF MUNDZUK. Yeah... Adjusting.

ILL *throws his hands up*. CHIEF MUNDZUK *and* PERCY *burst out laughing, throwing their hands up, exaggerated trembling*. ILL *runs away*.

Scene Three

Town hall. MAYOR HERCKHEIMER*'s office.* MAYOR
HERCKHEIMER *is at his desk, smoking a cigar. There's a gun
on his desk.* ILL *enters.*

MAYOR HERCKHEIMER. My boy.

> ILL *stares at the gun.*

> The panther.

ILL (*pointing at the cigar*). Henry Clay?

MAYOR HERCKHEIMER (*looking at the cigar*). Gift from a,
a –

ILL. I know who they're from. Didn't know you smoked.

MAYOR HERCKHEIMER. People are full of surprises! Some
surprises are more agreeable than others.

ILL. New necktie. Silk.

MAYOR HERCKHEIMER. Good eye! Trudie picked it out.
Mayor of a prosperous little city, got to look the part.

ILL. But we rejected her offer.

MAYOR HERCKHEIMER. It was the right thing to do, at the
time, in the heat of the –

ILL. So we're not prosperous.

MAYOR HERCKHEIMER (*flapping the tie*). It's aspirational.

ILL. I'm afraid.

MAYOR HERCKHEIMER. What of?

ILL. How can you ask me that? The town's gone credit-crazy.
We found a way of taking her money without admitting it.
I won't be around to take it, because you're going to
murder me.

> *Silence.* MAYOR HERCKHEIMER *looks down at his hands
> – or is he looking at the gun?*

MAYOR HERCKHEIMER. This town sacrificed plentitude for the sake of community – which goes hard against the American grain. But we did it. For you. You repay us by accusing us. I'd be shocked by your ingratitude, my boy, if certain facts about your character or lack thereof hadn't come to light.

WALLACE *enters with several huge boxes stacked on a dolly.*

WALLACE. The Remingtons!

ILL *stands up, terrified.*

MAYOR HERCKHEIMER (*to* ILL). Typewriters, not rifles!

(*To* WALLACE.) In the secretarial pool.

WALLACE *carts them off.*

It's sad to see you there, pale and quaking, all your sins exposed to daylight. You're a capable guy, you could've been my successor, but – Your rise and fall, it's like a Shakespeare tragedy.

ILL. Or Greek. I'll tell you what's rising and falling. What I did was bad, we all agree on that. But in your and everyone else's estimation, the let's-face-it fairly ordinary sins I committed forty-five years ago grow heavier and heavier with every passing minute – must be the weight of all that money! While killing me, everybody recognized that straight away, the heaviest sin there is, but it's somehow lighter and lighter the longer you have to wait for your paycheck! *I'm* sinking while she's rising up.

MAYOR HERCKHEIMER. We turned down a billion dollars because of you, and since you mention it, I don't call what you did ordinary; personally I don't know any man worthy of the name who's guilty of such rascality. Certainly no such man is worthy of elected office.

ILL. Ah.

MAYOR HERCKHEIMER. I'll keep the whole sordid affair out of the papers. Because of my friendship for you, which abides, undiminished, even though you're unfit for the position we'd previously –

ILL. What about the terms of her offer? The stipulation. Are you keeping that out of the papers as well?

Little pause.

MAYOR HERCKHEIMER. Can't squelch one story and not the other. So. I've seen to it, the *Slurry Democrat* and the *Erie Constitutional* both. Suppressed.

ILL. Uh-huh.

After I'm shot you'll say he thought it was the panther when he pulled the trigger –

MAYOR HERCKHEIMER. Who pulled what trigger?

ILL (*continued from above*). – and the papers will say it was a hunting accident.

MAYOR HERCKHEIMER. Want a gun of your own? Here!

He opens a drawer and pulls out another gun.

ILL. I don't want a gun!

MAYOR HERCKHEIMER. Then get a grip, boy! Give me the name of the person you suspect and I swear I'll investigate.

ILL. All of you. I suspect the whole –

MAYOR HERCKHEIMER. For shame!

ILL (*continued from above*). I don't *suspect*, I *know*! And so do you! None of you *wants* to be the one who does it. But somebody will!

BILL *rolls in an architect's scale model of a new town hall.*

BILL. Where do you want –

MAYOR HERCKHEIMER. OUT! TAKE IT OUT! I'M IN A MEETING!!

ILL *stops* BILL. *He looks at* MAYOR HERCKHEIMER, *then at the model.*

ILL. It's so... detailed.

BILL. Isn't it? Look in the windows, you can see little people and little desks and carpets.

MAYOR HERCKHEIMER. Even without her money, we can still afford to dream, can't we!? Or, or are you going to kill our dreams the way you've managed to kill any hope we had of seeing them realized?!

ILL (*squinting in at one of the windows*). Look, there's you! You're... (*Adjusting his angle.*) You're unveiling a bust, it's... (*Looking at* MAYOR HERCKHEIMER.) Is it her?

MAYOR HERCKHEIMER (*a shrug*). A benefactor. Someone to whom the town owes a debt. Of gratitude. I asked the architect to leave it... indeterminate. It could be anyone. It could be you.

ILL. You're, you're trading in futures now. My death's the commodity. You've sentenced me to death.

Second Interstitial

BOBY's *strapping on* CLAIRE ZACHANASSIAN's *Dresden china leg as she watches* ILL *leave the town hall.* BELSHA *is painting.*

CLAIRE ZACHANASSIAN. He's feeling it now, the whirlpool's spiraling pull, he's paddling frantically, poor ratty old cat. Nothing will save him, not all his might and main and mange and et cetera.

BOBY *stands; the leg is strapped in place.* CLAIRE ZACHANASSIAN *stands, tests it out.*

Well buckled, Boby.

BOBY *bows out.*

BELSHA. Those neo-realist film guys you're so smitten with are social realists just like me, but Italian men? I hear they're lousy in the sack. Marry me. I'm a phenomenal lover, I go the distance and I'm ambidextrous.

CLAIRE ZACHANASSIAN. Huh.

BELSHA. You want reality? I'm real.

CLAIRE ZACHANASSIAN. Are you? But #8 was my last, I won't marry again. My life's work is nearing completion, my every third thought shall be my grave, and my every first and second thoughts, someone else's. Not yours, you're dead already, Ashcan, a figurative oil painter – you're a prewar relic.

She stands.

BELSHA. The portrait! It isn't finished!

CLAIRE ZACHANASSIAN. Time is circular; it's finished before it's begun. And vice versa. And et cetera. Et cetera shares its roots with haetera. Did you know that, Ashcan?

BELSHA. A haetera's some kind of whore, no?

CLAIRE ZACHANASSIAN. Haetera, Et cetera: from Kai ta hetera, the remnants, the leftovers, the scraps and trash and garbage – hence haetera: Whore. Zachanassian diddled with Nazis; the Armenians were mostly anti-fascist but with Zachanassian business came first. And I diddled with him, hence… I diddled for survival of course, then… after surviving got settled, I took stock and realized I hadn't. Survived. I was what remains, the… consequences of what had happened that brought me to the house in Hamburg. After I met Zachanassian, who paid so well I could eat my fill, I came to understand my memory of hunger pangs as what remains of the remains of hunger, the ghostly traces of what I'd endured because of what he'd done to me, what they'd all done to me, so many hundreds of millions, so many billions ago. That ache, being immaterial, seemed to me immortal. Which was perhaps its path to becoming an understanding, larger-hearted, I think, than a mere story. I am the ghost of what happened, I am what remains of what happened. I'm memory.

I am, or I will become, a myth.

Scene Four

A churchyard outside REVEREND MESSING*'s church.*
REVEREND MESSING *is overseeing* BEDNEY *and* DAN
planting new bushes among the graves. ILL *approaches. He
stops when he sees that* REVEREND MESSING *holds a rifle.*

REVEREND MESSING. Be not afraid. I'm protecting my
    gardeners. The landscapers delivered prematurely; the
    rootballs mustn't be allowed to dry out, even when there's
    a wild predator about.

> BEDNEY *and* DAN *look nervously about.*

ILL. Reverend, you baptized my children, please, you've got
    to –

REVEREND MESSING. And I buried your parents. They're
    over… Now wait, where are…?

> REVEREND MESSING *swings about, looking for the
> graves, heedless of the rifle he's unaccustomed to carrying;*
> ILL, BEDNEY *and* DAN *duck for cover.*

ILL. Put down the gun!

REVEREND MESSING (*pointing with the rifle*). THERE!!!

ILL (*spinning wildly, expecting an attack!*). WHAT?!

REVEREND MESSING. Their mortal remains. Their souls rest
    in eternal repose. Can you say the same for your soul, Ill?

ILL. Help me! I'm in danger.

REVEREND MESSING. Your *soul* is in danger.

ILL. No, *I'm* in danger. You've got to, to listen to me!! My soul
    doesn't care if I'm living or dead, it'd probably prefer me
    dead so it can leave this awful town, but, but now that
    death's biding her time behind every door, now when I've
    never felt so, so *mortal*, I'm more sure than I've ever been,
    Reverend, that I do not want to be killed, not at all, not in the
    least bit. I want to live! Help me!

REVEREND MESSING. A man knows not what hour his Lord
    will come, my son, therefore –

ILL. WAKE UP!! SEE WHAT'S HAPPENING!! They're
preparing… heathen festivities, the golden calf, they're
armed, they've formed into teams, the girls are painting their
faces and shaving their legs, the boys are putting on gaudy
Hawaiian shirts, and rubbers in their pockets, their mothers
are clipping pearl earrings on, and the men are liquoring up,
and the whole godforsaken town's getting ready to eat out on
my corpse, I'm asking you for sanctuary, Reverend, please,
my terror is hell! I'm in hell.

REVEREND MESSING. Hell's in the heart. You abandoned the
poor girl, and you married a rich girl, and now you believe
everyone is as mercenary as you. Take stock of your sins, Ill.
Think only what *you* owe to your maker! He hath punished
us less than our iniquities deserve, and given unto us such
deliverance as this!

A bell begins to ring in the church steeple.

ILL. That's, that's a bell. A new…

REVEREND MESSING. It's good, isn't it? Such an
improvement over the old one. It's Austrian! And wait, wait
one more moment, it's…

A second bell, pealing higher than the first.

It's got a baby brother! It's like God's pure love made
musical, it sings of happiness unburdened by earthly cares –

A gunshot close by! ILL, REVEREND MESSING,
BEDNEY *and* DAN *fall to the ground.*

Ill! Ill! Run from us, save us, Ill, save us from sin!!! Don't
tempt us by remaining, Slurry is weak, we're weakened by
hunger, and wicked thoughts are emerging!! In the pealing of
that bell I hear the wailing of the damned, appealing to you,
pleading with you, take flight, board the very next train and
go, else you destroy us by making us murderers!

Several more gunshots!! During this, BEDNEY *and* DAN
crawl on their bellies towards the church.

BEDNEY. Mayday! Mayday!!

DAN. Head for the church, head for the church!!

The firing stops. ILL *leaps to his feet and starts to run, then stops, as* KOBY *and* LOBY *rise up from behind his parents' headstones.*

KOBY. The shooting is over, for now.

LOBY. For now. Poor panther.

KOBY. Poor panther won't anther.

ILL. It's…?

LOBY. It's dead. Fred. It's bleeding, it's –

ILL *runs out.*

KOBY. Bled.

KOBY *and* LOBY. Her poor panther's dead.

Scene Five

The train station, which, like everything else in Slurry, looks much better than before.

ILL *sits on a bench, waiting for a train, suitcase in hand. He looks dreadful, shaky and exhausted, his hollow eyes darting about, on high alert. He stares down the track, then at the station clock. He goes closer to the station clock, accurate because it's…*

ILL. New. Swiss. Jesus Christ. It's inhuman, how fast… the wheels turn. It happens so fast.

WALLACE, BILL, BEDNEY *and* DAN *enter.*

ALL FOUR MEN. Morning, Mr Ill.

ILL. Oh, um, good morning, I'm…

WALLACE (*a beat, then:*). Waiting for the Sirocco?

BEDNEY. Blasdell–Fredonia–East Palestine–Pittsburgh.

WALLACE. It's stopping here again.

BILL. Due any minute. Didja get a goggle at the brand-new clock?

DAN. Heading south, Mr Ill?

ILL. I need to, to get away from all this, this… change. I need to make a change. I'm done with everything, here, I was thinking I'll –

MAYOR HERCKHEIMER, MISS COVINGTON *and* DR NUTLING *enter, followed by several of the* AFTER-SCHOOL TUMBLERS. ILL *stares at them, and then says to* DAN:

Mexico, maybe.

DAN. As far south as that?!

MAYOR HERCKHEIMER. You could have told me you were planning to run off to, to – *Mexico*?

ILL. I don't have to tell you anything. I wrote a letter! So… People know. Keep back. Why did you follow me here?!

MAYOR HERCKHEIMER. A letter to who?

MISS COVINGTON (*over the above, to* ILL). If I may, I, I think that's inadvisable.

ILL (*over the above, to* MAYOR HERCKHEIMER). Governor Harriman, Special Post to Albany. I told him all of it, everything, so if – (*To* MISS COVINGTON.) What's inadvisable?

MAYOR HERCKHEIMER. Did he answer? The Governor?

MISS COVINGTON (*over the above, to* ILL). Mexico.

ILL (*over the above, to* MAYOR HERCKHEIMER). He didn't. Yet, but… (*Realizes something.*)

DR NUTLING (*over the above, to* ILL). *Turista.*

MISS COVINGTON. Intestinal parasites, yes, but also remember one of her eunuchs fled to Mexico. To no avail.

ILL. The postmaster.

MAYOR HERCKHEIMER. A trusted public servant. I won't have you disparage him.

ILL. I just saw him, driving a new Nash Ambassador. My letter never –

More SLURRIANS *arrive. In the distance, a train horn blasts. The* STATIONMASTER, *a new employee, comes out of the stationhouse in a spanking new uniform. He waves his flag as the train approaches, louder and louder.*

MAYOR HERCKHEIMER. Here's your train, Ill.

DR NUTLING. A happy healthy life to you, long as it lasts.

ILL. What's that supposed to – (*To the* SLURRIANS.) Stop crowding me!!

MISS COVINGTON. I don't think we are. I think we want you to get on your train.

ILL. Not all of you do!

MISS COVINGTON. Most of us – no, all of us want you to go. But some of us… also want to, to –

ILL. To murder me!

The squeal of the train's brakes as it pulls into the station, exhaling great clouds of steam, in which its CONDUCTOR *materializes.*

THE CONDUCTOR. SSSSsssssssiiiiiiiIIIIIIIIIIIrrrrrrrOCCO! Blasdell–Fredonia–East Palestine–Pittsburgh and all points south! AaaaaaAAAAAAAllaBOARd!

He returns to his train. ILL *clutches his suitcase, too terrified to move. The* SLURRIANS *face him, waiting.*

MAYOR HERCKHEIMER. Get on the train, Ill.

ILL. I can't!

MAYOR HERCKHEIMER. Who's stopping you?!

ILL. You will, if I move!! One of you, you'll grab me, and then somebody else will, and the rest of you will hold me so he can throttle me!

DR NUTLING (*to* MAYOR HERCKHEIMER). He sounds a little crazy.

ILL. *She's* crazy, and she makes the world a madhouse, and you've all taken leave of your senses. I'll get on if you'll let me, but, but you wouldn't have showed up like this, surrounding me, if... Why did you come?

MISS COVINGTON. Not to do you harm! With our destinies so bound up with yours. We... needed to see you, somehow, going or, or not going or –

ILL. You're goddamned liars, all of you are lying –

MAYOR HERCKHEIMER. You're the liar, it's your lies have dragged us into this morass! Get on board and good riddance!

ILL (*continued from above*). – not to me, to yourselves! You pray to God some other guy's gonna do it, but, but when you cash that check, there'll still be the truth and you'll have to live with it, you're praying to profit from murder!!

The CONDUCTOR *enters.*

THE CONDUCTOR. LlllAST call for BLASdell!!! LllllllAST call!

The CONDUCTOR *goes off.*

ILL. If I move, you'll kill me.

MAYOR HERCKHEIMER. That's your hypothesis. Now see if it holds. Get on board.

MISS COVINGTON. Stop this nonsense and snap out of it. Go!

ILL. Let me go!

MISS COVINGTON. How can we?! We aren't detaining you!

ILL (*continued from above*). Please, I'm begging, don't – You have guns!!

MAYOR HERCKHEIMER. Who's got a gun?! You're seeing things!!

ILL (*continued from above*). If I turn to run you'll shoot!! If I try to get on board you'll kill me, and you'll be rich but – If I don't get on the train you'll try to kill me, if not now, then soon, so – (*To the* SLURRIANS.) SAY SOMETHING! DO SOMETHING!! WHAT SHOULD I DO?!?!

A great blast of steam from the train. The STATIONMASTER *comes out of the stationhouse with a green flag. He raises it, waves it, swings it down. The train's horn blasts, steam billows forth one last time, engulfing the stage; and the train pulls out of the station.*

When the steam clears, ILL *is kneeling by his suitcase, head in his hands. The* SLURRIANS *are walking back towards the town.* MISS COVINGTON, WALLACE, BILL, BEDNEY *and* DAN *remain.*

MISS COVINGTON. No one prevented you from boarding. Only yourself.

Why?

She leaves.

BEDNEY. Calls to mind the words, 'My stronger guilt defeats my strong intent.'

BILL. Just so. 'And, like a man to double business bound – '

WALLACE. 'I stand in pause where I shall first begin – '

DAN. 'And both neglect.' Who among us has not been in that predicament?

But… trains don't wait.

ILL. I'm dead.

End of Act Two.

ACT THREE

Scene One

In Peterson's barn, boards missing from the walls, half the roof gone, exposing a black sky, allowing a huge hunter's moon to light up the barn's ruined interior. The hay bales have turned over many years into monstrous heaps of steaming, rancid mulch. A hayloft long ago collapsed under the weight of bloated bags of water-saturated oats; the bags are scattered across the barn floor, intact or burst open. Under the timbers of the hayloft, a crushed tractor rusts. Spiderwebs, some of outrageous diameter, glitter with night dew. In a corner, the skeleton of a cow, partially covered by moth-eaten hide.

In the midst of this, CLAIRE ZACHANASSIAN *sits on her sedan chair.* ROBY *leans against a post, playing 'Blute nur, du liebes Herz' from Bach's St Matthew Passion on his guitar;* DOBY *plays with matches.* MISS COVINGTON, DR NUTLING *and* REVEREND MESSING *face* CLAIRE ZACHANASSIAN.

MISS COVINGTON. For thirty-seven years I've taught at Slurry High, thirty-seven years' striving with every pedagogical skill I possess to nourish the barest most hesitant most vulnerable green shoots of humanist apprehension, praying to a heaven I truthfully no longer find entirely plausible –

REVEREND MESSING. Now then.

MISS COVINGTON. I can say that now, openly, let them fire me, I don't care.

CLAIRE ZACHANASSIAN. How will you live?

MISS COVINGTON. Mrs Zachanassian. You only arrived two days ago, but already your visit has taught me, a lifelong teacher of high-school students, who believed she'd seen the disheartening worst of human nature in its hordes of addle-pated adolescents, that our species is more available to depravity and savagery than are the animals we domesticate. Life as I understand it has been cheapened by your visit, your charity that mocks the origins of that noble word. Your munificence is a glass through which those of us who wish to may see our true selves, darkly. How will I live if they fire me. I'll sleep in an alley. I don't care.

CLAIRE ZACHANASSIAN. Yes, I see. Or maybe it's just the proximity to a billion dollars that's exciting dreams of freedom from necessity and liberating your despair, in which only the rich can really afford to roll about. Marx was right; Adam Smith was right; it boils down to money.

REVEREND MESSING. Oh but, but no, it, it doesn't! It –

MISS COVINGTON. She's right.

REVEREND MESSING. She's not! Pardon, dear lady, but you're wrong, she's wrong, I mean, look at us! Only Dr Nutling there makes anything you could call a living, and he makes very little –

DR NUTLING. Less and less.

REVEREND MESSING. And he's stayed, and Miss Covington has stayed, and I myself, well, here I am, in Slurry. We work day and night to, to cure poor people of rickets, to tend to the tubercular, to minister to the befuddled souls in their stricken, exhausted bodies, to try to teach their children the structures of thought so that the strictures of the Lord might mean something to them. Such suffering as we've seen has elicited such sacrifice! Not for money!

CLAIRE ZACHANASSIAN. Then for what?

REVEREND MESSING. Poor child. Why, for the reward of the Great and Glorious Hereafter!

CLAIRE ZACHANASSIAN. Reward's just a synonym for payment. You're working for your wages, or for profit, like everyone else. Toiling for a paycheck no one's ever seen anyone actually get, or get to cash in, that takes steady nerves, I guess, or stupidity.

MISS COVINGTON. I don't endure teaching's many hardships so I can go to heaven. I do it selfishly, not for my miserable salary, but as a long-term investment in my future life, which has credibility for me only to the extent that my immediate surrounding, my community has viability. If Slurry lives, and I have given to Slurry, I live. I'm not a fool. Had I believed, had any of us believed that Slurry is as irredeemably hopeless as a cursory acquaintance with its present paupery would lead one to suspect, I'd have gone elsewhere, and so would the doctor, and even you, Reverend. You stay because Slurry has vast hidden treasure. You're not a martyr, you're an investor. As are you, Mrs Zachanassian, you're a business woman, not a philanthropist, you haven't offered us charity, you've offered us employment: Ill's corpse is the commodity we're meant to produce for you. That's a meager return on a billion-dollar investment. What might that money generate if invested in our assets?

CLAIRE ZACHANASSIAN. You mean the factories.

MISS COVINGTON. The Wagner Works. Bockmann's Reverberatory Aluminum Manufactory. The Place-In-The-Sun Amalgamated Smelting Plant.

CLAIRE ZACHANASSIAN. Go on.

MISS COVINGTON. Buy them, invest in them. For ten million dollars, one one-hundredth of what you're offering, you can anticipate returns of a thousandfold, and Slurry will flourish without shedding blood –

CLAIRE ZACHANASSIAN. No bloodshed? Bet you've never worked in a smelting plant.

MISS COVINGTON. Don't quibble! I'm serious! The factories were bought for a song by some scrap-gathering vulture who's probably forgotten he owns them. You can grab them up for nothing! And so I say: Grab!

CLAIRE ZACHANASSIAN. It's an excellent idea.

MISS COVINGTON (*to* DR NUTLING *and* REVEREND MESSING). You see?! I knew she'd see the light of –

CLAIRE ZACHANASSIAN. Except it's too late. I can't buy the plants. I already did.

MISS COVINGTON (*uncomprehending*). You...?

CLAIRE ZACHANASSIAN. I own them.

MISS COVINGTON. Wagner's?

DR NUTLING. And Bockmann's?

REVEREND MESSING. And the Place-In-The-Sun?

CLAIRE ZACHANASSIAN. And this barn. And the fields outside. Every acre right up to the outskirts of Slurry, and the banks that hold the mortgages on every house and shop in town, which is to say the town in its entirety, I own it all. What with union costs and shipping costs and living standards and the transformation of America from a society of production to a society of consumption, I'm not sure you're right, schoolteacher, that your manufacturing plants have much potential, but whatever potential they had, I throttled it, I shut down the whole shitpile, deliberately. Your hope's a delusion, your patience was pointless, your sacrifices stupid, your lives, in fact, wasted. Useless.

Silence.

DR NUTLING. You're unnatural.

CLAIRE ZACHANASSIAN. It had been snowing for days, the day I left Slurry. I walked to the station in my schoolgirl's uniform, the nicest clothes I had, empty suitcase, baby in a blanket in my arms, slipping and stumbling, and the people of this town, *my town*, passed me by, and grinned at one another as you watched me go. The window on the train was glazed with ice, but I warmed it with my hand so I could watch Peterson's barn receding, and I think it was then that I said to myself, 'You'll be back.' Now I'm back. I own you all. I dictate the terms. There's nothing more to –

REVEREND MESSING. 'Though I speak with the tongues of
men and of angels, and have not charity, I am become as
sounding brass, or a tinkling cymbal. And though I have the
gift of prophecy, and understand all mysteries, and all
knowledge; and though I have all faith, so that I could
remove mountains, and have not charity, I am nothing. And
though I bestow all my goods to feed the poor, and though
I give my body to be burned, and have not charity, it
profiteth me nothing. Charity suffereth long, and is kind;
charity envieth not; charity vaunteth not itself, is not puffed
up, doth not behave itself unseemly, seeketh not her own, is
not easily provoked, thinketh no evil; rejoiceth not in
iniquity, but rejoiceth in the truth; beareth all things,
believeth all things, hopeth all things, endureth all things.
Charity never faileth: but whether there be prophecies, they
shall fail; whether there be tongues, they shall cease; whether
there be knowledge, it shall vanish away. For we know in
part, and we prophesy in part. But when that which is perfect
is come, then that which is in part shall be done away. When
I was a child, I spake as a child, I understood as a child, I
thought as a child: but when I became a man, I put away
childish things. For now we see through a glass, darkly; but
then face to face: now I know in part; but then shall I know
even as also I am known. And now abideth faith, hope,
charity, these three; but the greatest of these is charity.'

CLAIRE ZACHANASSIAN. Well done, windbag! I'm stiff
from the dampness! (*Calling.*) Doby! Roby! Take me back to
my room! (*To the three* SLURRIANS.) I own the hotel. In
case you were wondering.

As ROBY *and* DOBY *lift the chair and carry her out of the
barn:*

The Jacobeans bowdlerized it, windbag, you know this: In
the original Greek it isn't 'charity', it's 'love'. Charity
suffereth long, but love suffereth far far longer. Charity's
kind; love's anything but. Charity envieth not, but love does,
when he starts mooning after girls he hasn't ruined yet, and
he mumbles their names when he's fucking you, love envies.

Love vaunteth itself and gets puffed up because he loves you, you think, and love leads you to some highly unseemly places. Can't say that love isn't easily provoked: I fell in love with him head over heels in a single little instant, a heartbeat, one look and it was over, nothing in my life has ever been as easy as that. Charity thinketh no evil; I think I'm demonstrating what love thinketh. Charity rejoiceth not in iniquity; love's less pure. Charity rejoiceth in the truth; love rejoiceth too, except not in the truth that he never loved me at all. If that's true. Beareth all, believeth all, hopeth, endureth. See suffering, above. Charity never faileth. Love, once it fails, goes on failing forever.

She is gone.

DR NUTLING. Holy smokes, Pastor. What are we going to do?

REVEREND MESSING. Our best, Doctor. We'll do the best we can.

MISS COVINGTON. Will we? I wonder. I need a drink.

Scene Two

ILL's *general store has undergone a transformation. The floor is covered in fresh linoleum.* WALLACE, BILL, BEDNEY *and* DAN *are on ladders, installing a dropped ceiling of aluminum lattice and acoustic tile, with big fluorescent light fixtures humming and turning everything a merciless blue-gray, like in a morgue.* BELSHA *is scraping 'ILL'S GENERAL STORE' off the window and in the course of the scene will replace it with the outlines of a new sign: '24-7 GRAB AND GO™ '*

There's a new counter made of sparkly plastic, a new chrome cash register, lots of new merchandise on the shelves and stacked about on display tables. There's an electric chime that sounds when anyone enters or leaves the store.

MATTIE ILL *is behind the counter with a* SHOPGIRL *at her side. Both are in uniforms, 'Grab and Go' embroidered over their hearts.*

The door chimes as MR HOFBAUER *comes in, in a clean white shirt, bowtie, boldly checkered pants beneath a long butcher's apron, gory with blood.*

MR HOFBAUER. Carton of Camels, Mrs Ill, and an axe.

MATTIE (*alarmed!*). An axe?

MR HOFBAUER. A meat axe.

MATTIE *points to the items on the shelves; the* SHOPGIRL *fetches them.*

MATTIE. Back in business, Mr Hofbauer?

MR HOFBAUER. Now everybody's flush it's butcher's meat again.

The door chimes and MRS CREEKY *comes in.*

MRS CREEKY. Newspapermen! Worse than gnats! They'll chase you down one street and up another till you'll say anything, just to get rid of 'em. I hope I didn't say anything, I don't think I –

MR HOFBAUER (*to* MRS CREEKY). We ain't supposed to talk to 'em. The newspapers.

MRS CREEKY. I know! I said I don't think I – Anyway it's a free country and I can –

MR HOFBAUER. Chief Mundzuk's boy's been around to every store in town, warning against loose talk. I guess the kid's the Chief of Police now, which don't seem right given his age and what a little shit he always was but… It's so many changes in such a little while my bearings are all shot, like I'm tipsyish all the time even when I haven't tippled – I mean, this place for instance – (*The shop.*) just two days ago, empty shelves and the smell of termites at work, then presto-change-o, overnight it's –

MATTIE. We've been so busy, when the Grab and Go people came yesterday offering to, to partner with us, I couldn't see how not to, I just, I just didn't expect things would happen so fast!

MR HOFBAUER. It's like somebody dreamed it up! Sorta comes between you and, I dunno, reality or whatnot.

MRS CREEKY. Since she came calling. She's like a fog bank, rolling in and everything changes to blurry and gray.

MATTIE. She's very strange, but I can't help feeling… sorry for her. Hobbling around the planet like she does, looking for… something. Considering her life, she deserves some happiness.

MR HOFBAUER. He wrung her through the ringer like a dirty old mop, your husband did.

MRS CREEKY. Hofbauer!

MATTIE. It's alright. I know what he did.

MR HOFBAUER. The whole town knows it.

MRS CREEKY. And soon the whole country will know about it. The mayor's a ninny, thinking he could keep it quiet, a story like this! They want to talk to Ill, the newspapermen, and spit's on the griddle once they do! (*To* MATTIE.) Where is he?

MATTIE *looks up.*

He's still pacing?

MATTIE. Since he came back from the train station. Nonstop. Hasn't eaten since, sleepless too, and he won't talk to me, he… (*Starts to cry, then stops.*) Around and around the bedroom, like, like –

MRS CREEKY. We're all having a hard time with this, not just him. That's a lot of money. Even when I'm asleep, in my dreams, when I say 'one billion dollars' I can't help it, I laugh.

The door chimes and MISS COVINGTON *enters, drunk.*

MATTIE. I think Fred understands that what she said she wanted, that was just her emotional way of talking, to evoke for us what she'd been through, the depths of her grief.

MISS COVINGTON. I need alcohol, mighty alcohol. What've you got?

MATTIE. Scotch? Vodka?

MISS COVINGTON. Astonish me.

MATTIE *takes a bottle of vodka from under the counter.* MISS COVINGTON *opens it, swigs from the bottle.* MR HOFBAUER *whistles to get her attention.*

MRS CREEKY (*to the* SHOPGIRL). I'll take a dozen dinner napkins, ivory linen, and a carton of Chesterfields, Creeky likes Chesterfields best. And needles and an ashtray.

MR HOFBAUER. Don't mind if I –

MISS COVINGTON *hands him the bottle; he drinks, a mighty guzzle, and hands it back to her. She drinks and hands it back to* MR HOFBAUER, *who guzzles some more. The* SHOPGIRL *comes in with the items for* MRS CREEKY.

MRS CREEKY. I thank you. Charge it like always.

MISS COVINGTON (*to* MATTIE). Where is your husband?

MATTIE. Pacing. Upstairs.

MISS COVINGTON. Why not pace? Motion and mind, an essential duality. What was it Thoreau wrote? 'If you are ready to leave wife and child and friends and never see them again; if you have paid your debts, and made your will, and settled all your affairs, and are a free man; then you are ready for a walk.'

MATTIE. I think it's just to keep ahead of his terror, because motionless his fear catches him.

MR HOFBAUER (*now as drunk as* MISS COVINGTON). Nothing to fear, even though he's a bastard sonofabitch. NEVERTHELESS he's safe around here, safe as anyone can

be, what with the vicissitudes of – (*Picking up the cleaver.*)
Careful it's sharp. (*Waving it around.*) Careful, it's – Oh I said
that. I will situate myself here, at the door, to keep watch over
dear old Ill. (*To* MATTIE.) Ain't no other way he can get out,
is there?

The door chimes and CHIEF MUNDZUK *and* PERCY
come in.

MATTIE. Let me wrap that cleaver up for you, Hofbauer,
before someone gets cut.

MR HOFBAUER *raises his cleaver, rather wild-eyed.*
CHIEF MUNDZUK *pushes his arm down.*

CHIEF MUNDZUK. A reporter and a photog, right behind us.

MRS CREEKY (*to* MATTIE). Make sure he stays up there.

MATTIE. He will. He's afraid of you.

CHIEF MUNDZUK. He's nuts. It's us who're afraid – of him!
He starts raving about murder to the press, you think the old
lady will give us the billion? So nobody say anything, just
town's on the rebound, ain't it – Alley-oop!

TWINNINGS HOON, *a reporter for* Life *magazine, and his
photographer* ANTONY LEYVANHOUCK *enter.*

TWINNINGS HOON. Is this Alfred Ill's place?

MR HOFBAUER *raises his cleaver.*

(*To* MR HOFBAUER.) That's great! Hold that pose.
(*To* ANTONY LEYVANHOUCK.) Make sure you get the
hatchet.

ANTONY LEYVANHOUCK *takes a flash picture of* MR
HOFBAUER.

MATTIE. I'm Mrs Ill.

TWINNINGS HOON. Terrific. (*To* ANTONY
LEYVANHOUCK.) Get her and her daughter.

MATTIE. She isn't my –

The flash blinds her.

TWINNINGS HOON. Mrs Ill, how does it feel to know your husband almost married the world's richest woman?

MATTIE. At the moment, under the, the circumstances, it's sort of hard to, to… (*Again, she starts to cry.*)

TWINNINGS HOON. How about funny stories you want to share? About Mrs Zacha–

The door chimes and ZACHARY *comes in wearing a motorcycle jacket.*

MATTIE. That's my son, Zach– um, Zachary Ill.

TWINNINGS HOON. A good-looking boy! (*Confidingly to* MATTIE.) Does he know about, you know, the – (*Lewd waggling hand gesture.*)

MATTIE (*a cross between despair and anger*). Well, my God, who *doesn't* know?! What else is there to talk about?!

TWINNINGS HOON (*writing that down*). Wowee. That's – (*Touching his heart.*) OUCH! So, Zachary, what does it feel like, knowing that your dad could've married the richest woman on earth?

ZACHARY. Money's not the only thing there is. If she was my mom, I'd be someone else, and I'd rather be who I am than some guy named Zachary Zachanassian.

The door chimes and ANNALISE *enters, books under her arms.*

TWINNINGS HOON (*to* MATTIE). Your daughter?

MATTIE. A scholar!

ANNALISE. Stop it, Mom.

TWINNINGS HOON. A bookworm! (*To* ANTONY LEYVANHOUCK.) Make sure you get the school books.

(*To the rest of the* CROWD.) And you, Ill's friends, how's it feel that Claire Zachanassian hails from your very own town?

CHIEF MUNDZUK. On behalf of those assembled, I just wanna say how great we all feel about –

MISS COVINGTON (*lurching to her feet, swaying, pointing at* CHIEF MUNDZUK). I taught this man!

(*Pointing to* PERCY.) And him!

(*Then to* MR HOFBAUER.) Him with the axe!!

(MRS CREEKY.) Her with the napkins!!

TWINNINGS HOON (*to* ANTONY LEYVANHOUCK). Pictures! Pictures!

ANTONY LEYVANHOUCK *takes pictures.*

MISS COVINGTON (*continued from above, pointing to* MATTIE). And you!

(ZACHARY *and* ANNALISE.) And your children!

(*And the* SHOPGIRL.) And your shopgirl!

CHIEF MUNDZUK (*to* MISS COVINGTON). EXCUSE ME! You interrupted me! I was about to –

MISS COVINGTON. SILENCE, BOY! BACK TO YOUR DESK!!!

(*Climbs up with difficulty on a display table, upsetting the display.*) Sorry.

(*Sways atop the table.*) I STAND BEFORE YOU, AN HONEST WOMAN, WHO LIKE DIOGENES IN THE MARKETPLACE OR OR CHRIST IN THE TEMPLE I SHALL SPEAK THE TRUTH EVEN IF AT MY SPEAKING THE WITCH FLIES AWAY AND WE ARE LEFT SUNK IN POVERTY TILL THE END OF TIME!

CHIEF MUNDZUK (*to* MISS COVINGTON). Shut up! (*To* TWINNINGS HOON.) Don't listen to this souse, she's got three opinions about everything!

MRS CREEKY (*to* MISS COVINGTON). A teacher! And a lady! Drunken at midday! You oughta be sacked!

MATTIE (*to* MISS COVINGTON). Please come down, you'll fall and hurt yourself. You should be ashamed, in front of the children.

MISS COVINGTON (*to* MATTIE). They're your children, woman! You ought to be ashamed! Before the day ends they'll see their mother betray their father!

ZACHARY. Hey! Hey! I don't care who you are, nobody talks to my mother like that!

He tries to pull MISS COVINGTON *down, but she kicks and bats at him till he retreats.*

TWINNINGS HOON. Faster! Get her while she's – (*Imitating* MISS COVINGTON*'s flailing.*)

ANTONY LEYVANHOUCK. But what's going on here? I thought they were celebrating.

ANNALISE (*to* MISS COVINGTON). Please come down, you're humiliating yourself! They'll never let you talk!

TWINNINGS HOON (*over the above, to* ANTONY LEYVANHOUCK). Keep shooting!

ANTONY LEYVANHOUCK *does.*

MISS COVINGTON (*over the above, to* ANNALISE). YOU SHOULD JOIN ME NOT SILENCE ME! YOU ARE HIS DAUGHTER!

CHIEF MUNDZUK (*to* PERCY). Arrest her!

MR HOFBAUER (*waving his cleaver*). I can hack her to death with my brand-new meat axe!!

PERCY (*over the above, to* CHIEF MUNDZUK). But, but she's my English and Social Science teacher!

MISS COVINGTON (*continued from above*). OH GOD HELP THE COUNTRY WHEN THE YOUNG PEOPLE ARE SILENT AND THE OLD ARE THE ONLY –

ILL *enters from the back of the shop as* CHIEF MUNDZUK *and* PERCY *disarm* MR HOFBAUER. *As soon as they see him, everyone stops.*

ILL. What the hell's going on down here?

MISS COVINGTON. PERIPATEIA! ANAGNORISIS!
OEDIPUS IS PUFFED-UP LIKE A BLOATED OLD TOAD!
SUPPURATION LEADS TO ERUCTATION! I MEAN
ERUPTION! A VOMITING FORTH!

ILL (*weary, sad*). Yeah, okay. Now please get down from there.

MISS COVINGTON. You want me to… But, but Ill, Alfred
Ill –

TWINNINGS HOON (*to* ANTONY LEYVANHOUCK). It's
him! Shoot!

MISS COVINGTON (*continued from above*). – I must speak
out against this, against this –

ILL. Nobody asked you to say anything. Get down from there.

MISS COVINGTON. I'm, I'm a, a humanist, I read Latin, I've
read Plato in Ancient –

ILL. Get down. Atta girl. Get down now.

MISS COVINGTON *looks at* ILL, *as if trying to bring him
into focus. Then:*

MISS COVINGTON. Yes. Get down, humanism, down on the
ground.

(*Starts to get down, then turns to* ANNALISE.) Can you give
me a hand, dear? I'm a very very… drunk…

ANNALISE *helps* MISS COVINGTON *get down from the
table.*

…human being. (*To* ILL.) You're right. Why should I speak
for you, if you refuse to speak for yourself?

She slumps to the floor.

TWINNINGS HOON. The local drunk. Every town's got one.

Mr Ill, I presume?

ILL *looks at him.*

At last! Hoon from *Life*, *Life* magazine. If a good man is
hard to find, you must be a fricking saint! Thought the

town'd be doing a maypole dance with you as the pole,
but... I'm picking up on a certain grim, um –

ILL. We're unused to the attention. Makes us tense.

TWINNINGS HOON. You're tense alright! Just before you
came down, this guy (*Pointing to* MR HOFBAUER.) was
offering to hack the well-pickled old schoolmarm to bits!

ILL. But he didn't, did he? We're like a family, this town.
(*To* MR HOFBAUER.) Family? Isn't that so? You'd sooner
chop off your own hand than hurt a neighbor. Isn't that so,
Hofbauer?

MR HOFBAUER. Depends which neighbor we're talking
about. Can't chop nothing at present, 'cause Mundzuk and
Percy took my axe.

ILL goes to PERCY *and holds out his hand for the axe.*
PERCY *glares at him, then shrugs.*

PERCY. Your funeral.

He gives ILL *the axe.* ILL *gives the axe to* MR HOFBAUER.
ILL *and* MR HOFBAUER *look at each other.*

TWINNINGS HOON. Hey, let's do a comedy shot! Show the
readers how you guys clown around! Mr Hofbauer, raise the
cleaver high, right over Mr Ill's head.

TWINNINGS HOON *raises* MR HOFBAUER's *arm.*

Beautiful, and gimme some of that wild-eyed loony look you
had before.

MR HOFBAUER *distorts his face into a mask of homicidal
menace.*

Terrifying! (*To* ILL.) Mr Ill, look up at him, like, like he's
about to split your skull, like:

TWINNINGS HOON *demonstrates for* ILL *a look of terror.*
ILL *does his best to imitate it.* TWINNINGS HOON *corrals
the rest of* ILL's *family behind him.*

And you get over here, and you here, and the missus next to
her man.

Everyone does as they're told. ANTONY LEYVANHOUCK *gets ready to shoot.*

CHIEF MUNDZUK. Excuse me, Mr Reporter, I don't get what you're getting at, exactly, with this –

TWINNINGS HOON. Even with a globetrotting billionairess in your midst, you're people like people are everywhere. It'll humanize the –

He's interrupted by a sudden stream of many REPORTERS *and* PHOTOGRAPHERS *charging past the shop window, all in the same direction.*

What the...

BARNARD MENDELSOHNN, *reporter for the* Saturday Evening Post, *flings open the door, making the chime go crazy.*

BARNARD MENDELSOHNN. It's her! It's Zachanassian! In some kind of throne! They're headed for the woods!

BARNARD MENDELSOHNN *is gone, with* TWINNINGS HOON, ANTONY LEYVANHOUCK, CHIEF MUNDZUK *and* MRS CREEKY *following after.* ILL *and his family and* MR HOFBAUER *remain posed.* PERCY *stands by the door.*

PERCY. Take it easy, Mr Hofbauer. You're kinda in the presence of the law.

No one moves. MISS COVINGTON, *roused out of her stupor, has brought her eyes into focus enough to say, in quiet horror:*

MISS COVINGTON. Oh my God, oh my God, he's going to...

ILL. They're done. Now give me the axe.

MR HOFBAUER *and* ILL *stay posed,* MR HOFBAUER's *axe raised over* ILL's *head, for a VERY uncomfortable moment. Everyone in the store stares at them, no one breathing except* ILL *and* MR HOFBAUER; ILL *looks scared but also determined, perhaps resigned, while* MR HOFBAUER *looks like he might be considering striking* ILL *with the axe.*

Unless you plan to buy it.

The axe.

MR HOFBAUER (*not lowering the axe*). I'd like my Camels.

ILL *slides the carton of Camels over to* MR HOFBAUER.

ILL. In good health, Mr Hofbauer.

MR HOFBAUER. Charge it.

ILL. Naturally.

MR HOFBAUER *slowly lowers the axe. He walks towards the door.* MRS CREEKY *runs back in, snatches up her napkin press and runs back out, calling as she does:*

MRS CREEKY. House account! (*Exits.*)

MR HOFBAUER (*exiting*). If I can speak frankly, anyone who'd do what you did to Clara ain't no kind of gentleman.

PERCY *holds the door open for* MR HOFBAUER *as he says to* ILL *and the store:*

PERCY. He's a two-timing asshole is what he is.

As MR HOFBAUER *walks through the door:*

ILL. The axe.

MR HOFBAUER *looks at the cleaver, then at* ILL, *then flips the cleaver so he has it by the blade and the handle's extended. He hands it, handle-first, to* ILL, *and leaves the store.* PERCY *follows.*

MISS COVINGTON. So that's what your pacing revealed to you? Complicity in their madness?

ILL. It can't be madness when it makes transparent sense.

MISS COVINGTON. Wickedness, then.

ILL. But where'd the wickedness originate? Me. Who drove her crazy? I did. If she's crazy.

MISS COVINGTON. You sound like your friends who are going to murder you.

ILL. Yeah but unlike them I won't get paid for saying it, so
maybe what I'm saying is true. You want me to fight back so
you can feel good about people again. I can't help you. Or
myself. But what about them?

MISS COVINGTON. *Them?*

(*Stands, only a little unsteady.*) They're too poor to say no to
that much money. I'll go along. I'm becoming a murderer,
bit by bit. Before I attain maturity as a full-blooded
homicide, I retain my knowledge of a universal law: just as
the old lady came to call for you, she'll call for me, for us
all; and once we've done her bidding tonight, when she
comes for us, no one will help us. After tonight, I'll forget
that I ever knew that law, or any law other than hers.

Another quart of vodka, please.

ILL *puts it on the counter.* MISS COVINGTON *takes it.*

I'd like to open an account.

ILL. Done.

MISS COVINGTON *leaves the store.*

WALLACE. Should we keep working?

MATTIE. Stop for the day. We'll close up a little early.

MAYOR HERCKHEIMER *enters.*

MAYOR HERCKHEIMER. Who's got the Thunderbird
outside, parked in front of the fire hydrant?

ZACHARY. Shit.

ILL. You bought a car?

ZACHARY. A – Yeah, I – I just thought –

ILL. A T-Bird, huh?

So you can drive to wherever the road gang's working.

ZACHARY. It was on sale, installments, I figured one way or
another I'd figure how to pay for it.

ILL. Go move the car.

ZACHARY leaves, mortified. MAYOR HERCKHEIMER turns to MATTIE.

MAYOR HERCKHEIMER. Could you give Fred and me a moment?

MATTIE (*to the* MEN *on the ladders*). Come to the back, I baked shortbread.

The MEN *descend from the ladders and follow* MATTIE, ANNALISE *and the* SHOPGIRL *into the back.*

BILL. Shortbread's great but when're we ever getting paid?

BEDNEY. Be patient, just as soon as there's actual cash-in-hand cash.

WALLACE. And when's that gonna happen?

DAN. There's a time and a place for everything. Now shuddup.

MAYOR HERCKHEIMER and ILL are alone. MAYOR HERCKHEIMER takes a gun from his pocket. ILL steps back. MAYOR HERCKHEIMER puts the gun on the counter.

ILL. I still don't want one.

MAYOR HERCKHEIMER. There's a town meeting tonight at the Lake Erie Hotel.

ILL. I'll be there.

MAYOR HERCKHEIMER. We're in a bit of a quandary.

ILL. I get that. You are.

MAYOR HERCKHEIMER. There'll be television cameras from the big broadcast networks.

ILL. We're so interesting all of a sudden.

MAYOR HERCKHEIMER. Indeed we are. I issued a press release about you and Claire. How you were sweethearts once, it was you made her want to return to Slurry, how our circumstances, and you, Ill, persuaded the lady to an act of unparalleled generosity. How much we owe her. And you.

ILL. Thanks, I appreciate that.

MAYOR HERCKHEIMER. It wasn't for you I did that, I'm mad at you, Ill, but your family's decent as the day is long and no one wants anything but good for them.

ILL. Like I said: Thanks.

MAYOR HERCKHEIMER. We're putting it to a vote, no justices nor eunuchs nor anything unanticipated, thumbs up, thumbs down, accept the billion or don't. And what follows, follows.

ILL. Okay.

MAYOR HERCKHEIMER. It'll be hard on us all, either way the vote goes, and there's one way, I feel I must mention this, Ill, there's one possibility we haven't explored. If we could say to Mrs Zachanassian, before the meeting, that justice had been done, for her, by one of us, so we met her terms, but…

ILL. But?

MAYOR HERCKHEIMER. But say you took care of it yourself. (*Nods towards the gun.*) It's loaded. For us? For your town? Why force us to decide? Why force us into such an ugly confrontation with ourselves? Who needs that? Look at how much happier we are with money in our pockets. Not rich, but not frightened of eviction and – Couldn't you do it, as a gift to us? Wouldn't you feel better, knowing you'd spared us? And spared yourself?

Silence. ILL *looks at the gun. Then he pockets it.*

ILL. That… must've been hard for you to say to me. And… those are all good questions, your honor.

MAYOR HERCKHEIMER. What's the answer, my boy?

ILL. Guess we'll find out.

Scene Three

ILL *and his* FAMILY *in* ZACHARY*'s T-Bird,* ZACHARY
driving, in the countryside.

ILL. Notice how clean money makes things? Sweeps out the
gutters and puts paint on the houses and bees in the roses and
grapes on the vines in the arbors in the parks, flushes the
sewers and that helps the streams, and the fish in the streams,
and the little kids look better too, and the air smells like hope
and thins out towards the evening so the sounds of the
factory bells hang vibrating just a bit longer, singing quitting
time, home, supper and solace and a sweet night of rest.

ANNALISE. Oh look, Pop! It's a deer.

ZACHARY. Get outta the road, you!

He slows down, then stops.

ILL. Look at that.

ZACHARY. He's not budging.

MATTIE. He's not frightened.

ILL. Look at that.

ANNALISE. Fewer hunters these days, with the butcher back in
business, and the restaurants so busy. It's just like you said,
Pop. Money's an emolument.

MATTIE. I think you mean emollient, honey. But it's also
emolument.

ZACHARY. And monumental.

ANNALISE. And magical.

MATTIE. And there goes the deer!

MATTIE, ANNALISE *and* ZACHARY. So long, deer,
goodbye!

ILL. I'm getting out here, I'd like a walk, clear my head for the
meeting.

MATTIE. Will I walk with you, dear?

ILL. Not this evening. That okay?

MATTIE. It'll all be okay, dear.

ILL. It will. I know.

He gets out of the car.

ZACHARY. Wanna go to the movies? The new theater's opening. They're showing *East of Eden.*

ANNALISE. James Dean! Is the most!

MATTIE. I should go to the meeting.

ILL. No, you go with the kids.

MATTIE. But what if –

ILL. The movies.

MATTIE. Clairie's good-hearted. Yes, I'd like to see that picture. I think that she means well, she was nice, when she was young, when she... when we were at school, and what's really changed? Just money. So nothing that matters has changed. Fred... It gets cold in the forest. Are you dressed warm enough?

ILL. It'll all be alright.

He waves as they drive off. He walks into the forest.

Scene Four

The candlewood pines, twilight and darkening. ILL *sits on the ground, back against a fallen tree. He's looking at the gun. He opens the chamber, examines the bullets, spins the chamber, closes it, and then: He hears a noise among the trees. He peers into the darkness, immediately afraid.*

ILL. Who is it?! Who's –

A guitar plays a beautiful tune, twanging softly. CLAIRE ZACHANASSIAN *emerges from the darkness.* ILL *hurriedly pockets his gun.*

CLAIRE ZACHANASSIAN. That clicking – can you hear it?

ILL. What?

CLAIRE ZACHANASSIAN. It's southern pine beetles; they're killing the trees. They shouldn't be this far north, and yet – You can't hear them?

ILL. Not with the guitar playing.

CLAIRE ZACHANASSIAN. Mind if I sit?

ILL. They're your woods as much as they're mine.

CLAIRE ZACHANASSIAN. Actually – Nothing. Never mind.

She starts to sit, with difficulty. ILL *gets up and helps her. When he's lowered her onto the log, she holds on to his hands.*

Recognize the tune?

A beat, then ILL *smiles a little; he waits for the tune to return to the beginning, then:*

ILL (*singing*).
'Just a-wearyin' for you,
All the time a-feelin' blue,
Wishin' for you, wonderin' when
You'll be comin' home again.
Restless, don't know what to do,
Just a-wearyin' for you.'

CLAIRE ZACHANASSIAN (*singing*).
'Evenin' comes, I miss you more,
When the dark gloom's round the door,
Seems just like you ought to be
There to open it for me.'

ILL (*singing*).
'Latch goes tinklin', thrills me through – '

CLAIRE *and* ILL (*singing*).
' – Just a-wearyin' for you.'

CLAIRE ZACHANASSIAN (*produces a cigarette case, pops it open*). Smoke?

ILL. Please.

He takes two long black cigarettes from the case, puts them both in his mouth. She clicks a button on the side of the case, igniting a flame. She holds it to his cigarettes. He inhales, then exhales smoke. She closes the case, and lifts her chin, just a bit. He takes one of the cigarettes from his mouth and gently he puts it between her lips. They listen to the melody, smoking.

What color were her eyes?

CLAIRE ZACHANASSIAN (*a beat, then:*). I can't remember.

ILL. Hair?

CLAIRE ZACHANASSIAN. Black, wispy. An ordinary baby.

They sit for a moment, then:

ILL. Where'd she die?

CLAIRE ZACHANASSIAN. She was with people. I forget their names.

ILL. What happened?

CLAIRE ZACHANASSIAN. Meningitis, they said.

Now tell me about her mother.

ILL *looks at her.*

Do you remember her at all?

ILL. I think I do.

I've been pacing in my room, for a couple of days, I paced in a circle, round and round and I thought I was thinking how to escape, thought I was looking for an exit, a way out with my life. But my attention kept drifting to the center of the circle.

CLAIRE ZACHANASSIAN. Why?

ILL. A girl, a girl in a uniform, with a, a collar like on a sailor suit. Sixteen years old. A skinny kid. I could hardly believe… what a *kid* she was. And little. Not short but…

But breakably small. Didn't seem that way then, but now, with old eyes…

And she watched me, as I revolved around her, like she loved me, and I frightened her. I looked, I could've kept looking, forever, I hadn't remembered how it felt just to look at her, how looking I felt her come into me, through my eyes and into me, all the way to the back of my brain.

But I couldn't meet her eyes. Because I was afraid that she hated me, maybe, or still loved me, after all I'd done, or forgave me, or couldn't forgive me. Or she'd changed, or she hadn't. Or I was afraid she'd see me. And I'd hurt her even more.

They sit. The guitar's stopped. The forest is silent, except for a metallic clicking in the trees.

CLAIRE ZACHANASSIAN. Go back to town, Ill.

ILL. Can't I stay here?

CLAIRE ZACHANASSIAN. No. They're waiting for you there.

ILL. I could end it here. My purposeless life.

CLAIRE ZACHANASSIAN. But it has a purpose now, love. The purpose I've given you. To finish the story. Our story. This play I've composed. Your purpose is to help them to serve their purpose, and theirs to help you, and all for conclusion. Then I'll take you away, in your coffin, on a boat, and we'll sail the Aegean, in search of an island, with a grove of cypresses, cyclamen and dianthus, and I'll build a mausoleum there, will you stay there? With me.

ILL. What if, once I'm dead, you find you still hate me? Or love me? What if death doesn't end it for you?

CLAIRE ZACHANASSIAN. Someday I'll die.

Someday I'll die, but. Not so our story. It will be told and retold again and again until it grows so old it won't be old anymore, but immortal, revolving, the way the hands of the clock tell you that time passes and also that it never ends and starts again and again and again.

DOBY *and* ROBY *enter with the sedan chair.* ILL *stands up. They lift* CLAIRE ZACHANASSIAN *with great tenderness into the chair. Then they carry her away.*

Scene Five

The Grand Banquet Hall of the Lake Erie Hotel, grand as it ever was, maybe even grander. The town is assembling. Three huge television cameras, each manned by a CREW, *scan the hall. Three tweedy, avuncular newsmen –* DANA COWLE *of* CBS, BAT GORMLEY *of NBC and* JACK E. HOFFMANN *of ABC – headphones on, begin their broadcasts.*

DANA COWLE. And a grand evening to you, our TV viewers watching in your homes all across America. We're interrupting our regularly scheduled programming to broadcast live from the city of Slurry on the shores of Lake Erie in New York, the Empire State. Until recently, I reckon, few outsiders had ever heard of Slurry. It's no different from many of our country's small industrial towns: Sturdy, mostly modest houses, steeples of churches rising above beech trees, sycamores and maples; smokestacks of factories where copper and iron ore was smelted into ingots, where aluminum was manufactured and shipped westward across the lake, or eastward by rail or the Erie Canal.

Slurry is no different from hundreds of small American cities, except in one regard: Claire Zachanassian, the world's wealthiest woman, was born in Slurry, and two days ago, Slurry's homegrown billionairess came home, and what a homecoming this has turned out to be!

BAT GORMLEY. – the hall, traditionally used for concerts, operas and the local ballet is tonight the setting of a once-in-a-lifetime turn of events, unprecedented in my estimation, the kind of bolt-out-of-the-blue improbability you find in fairy tales and sentimental novels and well, it's just overwhelming, isn't it?

JACK E. HOFFMANN. – of one billion, you heard that right, that's Billion with a B. That's what Mrs Zachanassian has offered the town of Slurry, and tonight, this down-on-its-luck little township is gathering to vote on whether or not they're going to accept her princely and unprecedented tribute to the town where she was born. And you heard that right too, ladies and gentlemen: The town of Slurry is going to vote on whether to accept the billion. In most places such an exercise would be deemed unnecessary, but –

DANA COWLE. As it's been explained to me by Mayor Herckheimer, these good people hold steadfastly to the Jeffersonian ideal of direct participation for all enfranchised Slurrians, whose responsibility it is to settle civic affairs of consequence by means of a town meeting such as the one we will be witnessing tonight.

JACK E. HOFFMANN. Ladies and gentlemen of the viewing public, the Mayor of Slurry is mounting the dais and – There's a, an almost tomb-like silence in the hall, they're –

MAYOR HERCKHEIMER. Welcome, citizens. Since Slurry's founding, one hundred and eight years ago, we've met as a community to address issues of importance, openly, democratically. As your mayor, I call this meeting to order. There's one item on tonight's agenda, and we all know what it is. Claire Zachanassian, Dan Mucker's daughter, born here among us, and recently returned – is she here tonight? Clairie? Are you… ?

He surveys the hall, as do all the SLURRIANS *and the TV cameras, but she doesn't appear.*

A true philanthropist, less interested in applause than in the good she can do. It's my privilege to announce that Mrs Claire Zachanassian wishes to make a donation to the town of Slurry and its inhabitants of one billion dollars –

The SLURRIANS *don't react, but the* TV NEWSMEN *leap in front of the cameras.*

DANA COWLE. And if the almost-unencompassable amplitude of Mrs Zachanassian's conferment isn't an affair of consequence, I don't know the meaning of the word. The atmosphere in the hall tonight is tense but hopeful, concentrated rather than jubilant, determined yet –

MAYOR HERCKHEIMER *steps aside as* MISS COVINGTON *approaches the podium. She's made an unsuccessful effort to look presentable, she's green, unsteady, unwell, shielding her eyes from the glare of the TV lights.*

JACK E. HOFFMANN. Oh, oh wait, wait now, the mayor is, he's –

DANA COWLE. He's handing the podium over to the principal of the local high school, Mrs… (*Embarrassed laugh.*) Hah! Don't get mad at me, all you teachers watching out there, I don't seem to have the lady's name, but – (*Whispering.*) Let's give a listen.

MISS COVINGTON. I don't suppose it'd be possible to dim those rather… scourging lights? Out of pity for an old woman with the most dreadful headache…?

Oh never mind, I deserve no pity.

My friends, and my many former pupils. Before we vote, I've asked to address you. In exchange for this privilege I've agreed to state for the public record that Mrs Zachanassian has made no stipulations to the recipients of her largesse.

She sways slightly, as if about to topple sideways. MAYOR HERCKHEIMER *moves to steady her but she angrily waves him away and grips the podium to steady herself, saying under her breath as she does:*

Less difficult to say that than I'd imagined.

There are no stipulations imposed by our benefactress, but I feel that doesn't mean her gift is without meaning. It has a meaning, it has a purpose; the consequence of her billion-dollar donation, she hopes, is that justice will establish its residence in Slurry. This poetic demand demands that we reflect: Does justice dwell among us?

WALLACE. No!

BILL. We permitted a crime!

BEDNEY. We coddled injustice!

DAN. We countenanced perjury!

MRS BALK. We just didn't care!

MRS CREEKY. Couldn't be bothered!

MR HOFBAUER. Made pals with a bastard!

MR EMERSON. A rotter! A shitheel!

Some consternation among the CAMERA CREWS.

MISS COVINGTON. People of Slurry: money has only the meaning humanity assigns it. Poverty may have blinded us to the presence of injustice. But prosperity alone can't rectify wrongs. Money buys justice only when just men possess it. I implore you, should you decide, should we decide to accept her gift, that we simultaneously pledge ourselves to being worthy of it, to the task of remaking ourselves into vessels for the meaning of the money, rebuilding ourselves as we rebuild our town! Let's hunger for justice and not just deserts lest we, lest our hands remain stained by...

She's overwhelmed, burying her face in her hands, starting to weep. Tremendous applause. She runs from the podium.

DANA COWLE. It's like – I was just saying to my producer, it's like William Jennings Bryan on the gold standard, or Lincoln at Gettysburg, or Churchill or – oh wait, wait, things are happening fast now, and the mayor is calling for –

MAYOR HERCKHEIMER, *back at the podium, motions for silence, which comes immediately.*

MAYOR HERCKHEIMER. Now I ask that before we vote to cast our lot with justice, let's do right by one man, the single man most responsible for the great lady's gracious gift. Alfred Ill, please come forward.

A long wait in silence, except for the TV NEWSMEN, *speaking quietly to their cameras:*

DANA COWLE. Alfred Ill, as you know, Claire Zachanassian's high-school Romeo, is now a well-preserved man of about seventy –

BAT GORMLEY. – an old-fashioned Western New Yorker, hard-working, civic-minded, a neighbor with a good fence and a heart of –

JACK E. HOFFMANN. – averse to publicity, this servant of his community takes quiet satisfaction in – okay, okay, they've, they've coaxed him out, flushed him out into the limelight and –

ILL *has been more or less pushed to the front of the* CROWD, *facing the dais.*

MAYOR HERCKHEIMER. We owe this night to you, Ill. You understand that, don't you.

ILL *either mumbles or doesn't respond.*

MR HOFBAUER. LOUDER!

MAYOR HERCKHEIMER. Could you speak up a bit, my boy, the TV mics –

ILL. Yes.

MAYOR HERCKHEIMER. And when Slurry casts its vote to take Mrs Zachanassian's money, or not, will you accept that decision, and abide by it?

ILL. I understand it.

MAYOR HERCKHEIMER. Anyone present have anything to add? To ask Mr Ill?

Silence.

Alright then. All for justice, raise your hands.

Everyone except ILL *raises their hands.*

DANA COWLE. It's it's like a, a wheatfield of human hands, raised to the sun. Only the old man who worked hardest to

ensure this night might come, only he sits, hands folded – Is
he praying? Thanksgiving? Or is he overwhelmed with joy?

MAYOR HERCKHEIMER. The Claire Zachanassian/City of
Slurry Irrevocable Trust is born forthwith!

Prolonged cheering. Hats in the air. Confetti.

Not for the money!

SLURRIANS. Never just for money!

MAYOR HERCKHEIMER. Just for justice's sake!

SLURRIANS. For the sake of justice!

MAYOR HERCKHEIMER. And our consciences guiltless!

SLURRIANS. And our consciences free!

MAYOR HERCKHEIMER. To live the way money does!

SLURRIANS. Live the way money lives!

MAYOR HERCKHEIMER. Unchanged by happenstance!

SLURRIANS. Unchanged by happenstance!

MAYOR HERCKHEIMER. Impartial and rational!

SLURRIANS. Impartial and rational!

MAYOR HERCKHEIMER. Like God here among us!

SLURRIANS. God's here among us!

ILL (*a scream of grief*). GOD!!!! STOP!!!

DANA COWLE. Wait wait oh, oh shit – sorry – the fucking –
sorry, sorry, but, did we – did we get that?

Her CAMERA CREW *shakes its head.*

Your honor, I'm sorry. Something, some gear or something
in this piece of – two years old and already it's falling apart!
Can we do that again?

MAYOR HERCKHEIMER. The whole thing? Again?

DANA COWLE. Yeah, if you don't mind. For the people
watching on their TVs at home.

MAYOR HERCKHEIMER. Sure.

(To the SLURRIANS.) Ready?

SLURRIANS. YES!

MAYOR HERCKHEIMER. That's the Slurry spirit!

The CAMERA CREWS *do 'lights, action, roll!' and then:*

The Claire Zachanassian/City of Slurry Irrevocable Trust is born forthwith!

Again: prolonged cheering, hats, confetti.

MAYOR HERCKHEIMER. Not for the money!

SLURRIANS. Never just for money!

MAYOR HERCKHEIMER. Just for justice's sake!

SLURRIANS. For the sake of justice!

MAYOR HERCKHEIMER. And our consciences guiltless!

SLURRIANS. And our consciences free!

MAYOR HERCKHEIMER. To live the way money does!

SLURRIANS. Live the way money lives!

MAYOR HERCKHEIMER. Unchanged by happenstance!

SLURRIANS. Unchanged by happenstance!

MAYOR HERCKHEIMER. Impartial and rational!

SLURRIANS. Impartial and rational!

MAYOR HERCKHEIMER. Like God here among us!

SLURRIANS. God's here among us!

Silence. All eyes on ILL.

DANA COWLE. Um, isn't he…? Mr Ill, could you do that thing you did, before? When you… (*To* MAYOR HERCKHEIMER.) Could you ask him to… just for the, we can splice it together so –

MAYOR HERCKHEIMER. Ill? Could you say 'My God' for the cameras?

ILL *shows no sign of having heard any of this.*

DANA COWLE. OOOooooKAY! Some things you just gotta be there for! But it's fine! That's a wrap!

The CAMERA CREWS *immediately start disassembling their gear.*

MAYOR HERCKHEIMER. The buffet dinner for the town and our guests is right out through the doors there, in the Lake Erie Steakhouse, right off the lobby. A few of us will linger, the clean-up detail. So if you could, please head for the doors.

The CROWD *leaves.* ILL *suddenly moves towards the door.* CHIEF MUNDZUK *and* PERCY *are there to block him.*

CHIEF MUNDZUK. Stay.

ILL. Tonight? Here?

CHIEF MUNDZUK. What's it matter?

ILL. I'd rather be… home, so that it looked, you know, wouldn't it be easier to –

CHIEF MUNDZUK. You worry too much. We've worked it all out.

The auditorium is now empty, except for MAYOR HERCKHEIMER, MISS COVINGTON, REVEREND MESSING, DR NUTLING, MR HOFBAUER, MR EMERSON, CHIEF MUNDZUK, PERCY, WALLACE, BILL, BEDNEY *and* DAN. *And* ILL.

MAYOR HERCKHEIMER. Lock the doors, please.

MISS COVINGTON. Locked.

MAYOR HERCKHEIMER. Maybe turn off the lights.

The lights go out. Moonlight lights the hall.

So, let's see. Form a gauntlet.

The MEN *form a gauntlet, with* ILL *at one end. At the other end, a young* GYMNAST *appears. He flexes his arms, limbers up his hands.* REVEREND MESSING *goes to* ILL.

REVEREND MESSING. I'll pray with you, Ill.

ILL. Please don't.

REVEREND MESSING. I'll pray for you then.

ILL. Pray for Slurry.

REVEREND MESSING. God have mercy on our town.

ILL. There's no God here.

REVEREND MESSING. Oh. Oh but you're wrong.

REVEREND MESSING *joins the gauntlet.* CHIEF MUNDZUK *goes up to* ILL *and grabs him, violently by his shirt, tearing it.*

CHIEF MUNDZUK. Wanna pray now, you godless piece of shit?!!

MAYOR HERCKHEIMER. Stop!! What are you doing?!?!

CHIEF MUNDZUK. Oh, sorry, I just – Sorry, Ill. Force of habit. I got carried away. Damn.

MAYOR HERCKHEIMER. My boy? Are you ready?

ILL *cocks his head, as if hearing something.*

That's a rhetorical question, I suppose. It's time. Could you – Walk among us, Alfred Ill.

ILL *starts, then freezes, unable to move.*

CHIEF MUNDZUK. Move it.

ILL *resumes walking, down the center of the gauntlet, towards the* GYMNAST. *The gauntlet moves together, surrounding him. Midway, he falls to his knees. The gauntlet becomes a cluster of* MEN'*s backs; it contracts towards its center for a long moment, seems to pulse like a beating heart, then it stops moving.*

Then WALLACE, BILL, BEDNEY *and* DAN *leave the cluster, go to the doors and open them.* TWINNINGS HOON *comes in, then* DANA COWLE *and* BAT GORMLEY.

BAT GORMLEY. What's… What's happening in here? Who turned off the –

The lights are back on, blindingly bright.

The cluster of MEN *moves apart.* ILL*'s body lies on its back, eyes closed, hands folded. The* TV NEWSMEN *gather near.*

Oh my God.

DANA COWLE. Is he…?

DR NUTLING. Heart attack.

MAYOR HERCKHEIMER. Taken in his joy.

One of the four MEN *cover* ILL*'s body with the kind of plastic red-and-white checkered tablecloths found in pizza parlors.*

BAT GORMLEY. That's – Unbelievable. What an ending. Sorry, that was crass, it's just –

DANA COWLE. Can't beat life for stories.

Everyone turns because CLAIRE ZACHANASSIAN *has entered, on foot, followed by* BOBY *the butler, followed by the town of Slurry, which hangs back near the exits as* CLAIRE ZACHANASSIAN *approaches the covered corpse of* ILL.

She stands over him.

CLAIRE ZACHANASSIAN. Boby. Uncover him.

BOBY *casts the tablecloth aside.*

CLAIRE ZACHANASSIAN *looks at* ILL *for a long time, immobile.*

You look just like you did the day I first saw you, so long ago. Come away, sweet boy, my poor panther. It's time now; let's begin.

The coffin, Boby.

BOBY *looks at one of the doors. The* SLURRIANS *standing there part to make way for the four strong women* PALLBEARERS *in their black veils, carrying the coffin. At another door,* ROBY *and* DOBY *enter with the sedan chair,* KOBY *and* LOBY *following behind them, smiling, holding hands.*

The PALLBEARERS *walk to* ILL's *corpse, place the coffin on the ground, open its lid, and, confidently, respectfully, raise up* ILL *and place him in the coffin.* KOBY *and* LOBY *peer blindly inside. The* PALLBEARERS *close the lid and effortlessly lift the coffin. From yet another door, the endless procession of* FRENCH MAIDS, *carrying suitcases, each with a funeral wreath under an arm.*

CLAIRE ZACHANASSIAN *is raised up in her sedan chair.* BOBY *beckons to* MAYOR HERCKHEIMER *to approach the chair. When he's below her,* CLAIRE ZACHANASSIAN *reaches down to him and hands him…*

The check.

MAYOR HERCKHEIMER *stares at the check, and the* SLURRIANS *gather to watch as* CLAIRE ZACHANASSIAN *and her* ENTOURAGE *depart.*

The End.